# Introduction

It is not only children
who love sweet things and candies . . .
adults take great pleasure in eating them too. Among the many exciting
recipes and ideas we have chosen, there is a delicious selection for you to choose
from that will delight young and old alike . . . from lollipops and
toffee apples to truffles and *petit fours*.

Making your own sweets [candies]
and confectionery is surprisingly easy and inexpensive and also fun!
Give yourself a double treat – something delicious to eat and
fun to prepare.   We will show you how with
step-by-step instructions.

There are very few people
who would not be pleased to receive a special gift you have made
yourself – family, friends, the old or lonely, someone who is sick – all
will be delighted with your unusual and original present. Sweetmeats, made by
you, have such individual and different flavours – qualities all too rarely found in
store-bought alternatives. There are almost endless occasions when the gifts
of sweets [candies] and confectionery is the perfect answer; not only for
Thanksgiving, weddings, birthdays and anniversary celebrations
but also for a local garden fete, 'bring and buy' or P.T.A. sale,
your contribution to a party, congratulations
on graduation or 'passing a driving test', and
any other special occasion.

We will show you not only
how to make these mouth-watering confections but also
how to present them attractively. So take this opportunity to make the most
of your talents as a confectioner and satisfy
those sweet-toothed cravings!

I

# Basic know-how and equipment

Each of the recipes we give you has its own list of special ingredients and requirements, but there are some tins, spoons and measuring implements common to most and always handy to have at your elbow. These we have listed below plus a few useful hints and ideas to cut down on preparation times.

**Tins**
24 x 30 cm [9 x 12 in] tin
15 x 15 cm [6 x 6 in] tin
20 x 20 cm [8 x 8 in] tin
15 x 20 cm [6 x 8 in] tin
28 x 18 cm [11 x 7 in] tin
18–20 cm [7–8 in] square tin
Several baking trays
Baking sheet
Cooling tray/wire rack
Airtight tins and containers
for finished products

**Pans**
Medium-sized saucepans
Double saucepan (jellied sweets [candies])
Large, deep, heavy-gauged saucepan with straight sides that will conduct and maintain heat evenly (sugar-boiled sweets [Hard-candies])
Deep-frying pan

**Spoons**
Tablespoons
Teaspoons
Soupspoons
Slotted spoon
Wooden spoon
Spatula
Wooden fork

**Knives**
Sharp knife
Round-bladed knife/flat-bladed knife
Palette knife/metal sugar scraper
Cutting wheel
Shaped biscuit [cookie] cutters
Skewer
Scissors
Small fondant cutters

# How to make
# SWEETS AND
# CONFECTIONERY

to Di,
Best wishes, Christmas 1982,
love Jane
xxx.

**CAVENDISH HOUSE**

Do you remember the days before pre-packaged sweets and candies, when each and every one was individually hand-made with pure and natural ingredients and rows of gleaming jars and bottles contained mouth-watering delights?

Now you can revive those treasured skills by making individual confections for yourself that will surpass any store-bought alternatives: from toffee apples and humbugs to connoisseur confectionery like truffles and marrons glacés.

All the recipes are tried and tested and beautifully illustrated with step-by-step instructions, so there is no excuse for cries of 'I can't!'—It's easy as well as fun to do. Our basic know-how section will tell you all about the equipment you will need, plus handy hints on safety and preparation to aid both the inspired beginner and the expert.

We also show you how to present and package the goodies you will have made, for that extra special present.

When you have become really expert you can even turn your talents into a commercial enterprise!

Start now on one of your favourites, you'll be delighted with the results and your family and friends will be flocking to sample your new specialities. Whether you are making confectionery for your children or as unusual gifts, you will spend many happy hours creating works of culinary art.

**Edited by Jackie Cunningham-Craig**
**Designed by Carol Collins and Steve Leaning**
**Illustrations by Ann Rees**

Published by Marshall Cavendish Books Limited
58 Old Compton Street, London W1V 5PA.

© Marshall Cavendish Limited 1973, 1974, 1975, 1976, 1982

First printing 1976 (softback)
Second printing 1982 (hardback)

ISBN 085685 908 7

Printed and bound by L.E.G.O., Vicenza, Italy

**Important:** NB American terminology is indicated in the text by [ ] brackets.

# Contents

## Brushes
Medium fine brush ⎤
Finely tapered brush ⎬ Art supplies
2 bristle pastry brushes ⎦

## Paper
Grease proof paper/waxed paper
Rice paper
Card/paper
Aluminium foil
Polythene/polythene bags
[plastic/plastic bags]
Cocktail sticks
Wooden meat skewers/lollipop sticks
Set square

## Moulds
(For ornamental painted biscuits
[cookies])
are difficult to obtain so either:
make biscuits [cookies] without
or
make own clay moulds
or
use butter moulds

## Bowls
Heat proof bowl
Various-sized mixing bowls
Pastry-board
Cold working slab – preferably
marble or some other hard cold
surface – (sugar boiled sweets
[Hard-candies])
Rolling pin
Cups
Jug
Saucers – (for mixing vegetable dyes
for colouring)
Damp cloth

## Miscellaneous
Wire whisk
Electric whisk/spare pair hands
Forcing bag and plain icing tube
Mincer [grinder]
Grater
Food mill/blender
Sugar thermometer

# Handy hints and safety first

## Safety first

When cooking 'safety precautions' are essential to avoid 'accidents' and to make sure success is achieved every time.

1. Adult supervision is essential at *all* times when small children are cooking.
2. Small children should *not*, of course, be permitted to heat ingredients on the stove or put trays into or remove them from the oven themselves.
3. Sharp implements such as knives and scissors should also *not* be used by small children without adult supervision.
4. It is much safer to turn pot handles to the side of the stove in order to prevent unpleasant accidents.
5. Always use proper oven gloves when you are putting things into the oven and taking them out again.
6. It is, of course, important to use *edible* dyes not paints to colour biscuits [cookies] and sweets [candies].
7. Crystallized and glace-fruit should be soaked in warm water before use. Rub off excess sugar and dry thoroughly with a clean cloth.
8. Sugar-boiled sweets [Hard-candies] require special equipment and, because of the high temperature involved, you should be very careful when making them. Under *no* circumstances whatsoever should children be allowed near the pans.

## Handy hints

There are some basic things which every 'good cook' should know before beginning any cooking. Most of you will be aware of these – but it is still useful to be reminded of them once again!

1. Be sure to read the recipe all the way through before you begin cooking.
2. It will make things easier if you lay-out and weigh out your ingredients before you start cooking.
3. Clean hands are essential when cooking.
4. It is useful to wear an apron or overall when cooking in order to keep clothes clean.
5. If you wash up as you go along it will make it easier for you.

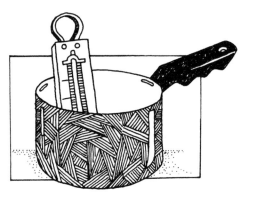

# Sugar boiling

Sugar boiled sweets [Hard-candies] like lollipops and humbugs [Hard-candies] require special attention and equipment so we will give you a few useful hints.

You will need a large, deep, heavy-gauge saucepan with straight sides that will conduct and maintain heat evenly, two bristle pastry brushes – one for washing down the sides of the pan and the other for oiling, a scrupulously clean wooden spoon, a palette knife or a metal sugar scraper, a cold working slab – preferably marble and last, a sugar thermometer is very important.

Check the thermometer for accuracy by placing it in a pan of water and bringing to the boil – when the water boils, the thermometer, held at eye level, should read 100°C [212°F].

It is very important to measure sugar and water accurately. Too much water means the syrup takes longer to reach the required temperature with the result that the syrup discolours. Too much sugar is difficult to dissolve before water reaches boiling point.

Always stir the water and sugar very gently over very low heat to help dissolve the sugar. Every grain must be fully dissolved and stirring stopped before boiling point is reached.

Keep a pan of hot water beside the sugar boiling pan. Use it to hold your thermometer, wooden spoon and a pastry brush.

Frequently wash down the inside of the saucepan with the hot wet pastry brush. This is to brush back into the liquid any crystals that form just above the water level. (If necessary, continue washing down after the syrup boils.)

When the sugar solution boils do not stir the mixture unless specifically directed to do so by the recipe as this causes grainy mixture.

Place the warm thermometer (a cold one might shatter) in the syrup pan.

When the desired degree is reached, carefully remove the syrup pan from the heat and replace the thermometer in the hot water pan.

## Teaspoon testing

Although less desirable, it is possible to make some sugar boiled sweets [Hard-candies] without a sugar thermometer. In this case temperature is tested by dropping half a teaspoon of the sugar mixture into a cup half-filled with cold water. The condition of the rapidly cooled sugar acts as a temperature gauge (as indicated on the sugar boiling table given). Naturally this method of testing is considerably less accurate.

**Short thread** means that the cooled sugar will feel sticky to the fingers and will form a short thread when the thumb and forefinger are pulled apart.

**Long thread** means the syrup is slightly more tacky and a longer thread can be formed when finger and thumb are pulled apart.

**Soft ball** means that the cooled sugar forms into a small very malleable ball.

**Hard ball** means a firm but still malleable lump of sugar is formed.

**Crack** means that, as soon as it enters the water, the cooled sugar sets into a brittle thread which will bend and break.

**Hard crack** means that the brittle thread formed snaps without bending.

**Caramel** means the colour of the sugar solution turns to light gold, then to deep brown and the cooled sugar is very brittle and breaks easily.

## SUGAR BOILING TABLE

| Temperature | Description | Use For |
|---|---|---|
| 102°–104°C [215°–220°F] | Short thread | Thin syrups |
| 107°–110°C [225°–230°F] | Long thread | Thick syrups |
| 115°C [240°F] | Soft ball | Fondants and soft fudges |
| 118°–121°C [245°–250°F] | Hard ball | Hard fudges |
| 155°C [310°F] | Crack | Soft toffees |
| 163°C [325°F] | Hard crack | Hard toffees and spun sugar |
| 193°–199°C [380°–390°F] | Caramel | Coating fruit, gateaux and cakes, also as a colouring agent for savoury sauces |

5

# Simple everyday treats

Every parent is familiar with the problems of pocket money and the never ending children's cry of money for sweeties [candies]. How much nicer it would be to have a store of inexpensive, delicious sweets [candies] to pop into your child's lunch box or for a mid-morning treat. Most mothers know that feeling, after the house-work is finished and she stops for a cup of coffee, when a little something sweet is just what she would like. Now she will be able to indulge herself.

This chapter will show you how to make exciting yet simple, small sweets [candies] for adults and children alike – from lollipops and toffee to marshmallows and fudge. If you follow the instructions carefully for storing and wrapping you will always have a selection for those weak moments, to pop into a bag or even wrap up for that special last minute present. So why not treat yourself and have something special everyday!

# Lollipops, barley sugar and jellies

Lollipops, barley sugar and jellies [Gum drops], three time-honoured favourites remembered and enjoyed by all.

### Almond brittle lollipops
Attractively shaped and nicely textured, these lollipops are a treat to suck or chew.

| You will need: | Metric/UK | US |
|---|---|---|
| Sugar | 225gm/8oz | 1 cup |
| Well rounded tablespoons golden syrup [light-corn] | 2/2 | 2 |
| Water | 75ml/3fl oz | $\frac{3}{8}$ cup |
| Liquid glucose (teaspoon) | 1/1 | 1 |
| Butter | 15gm/½oz | 1 tbsp |
| Chopped almonds | 50–100gm/ 2–4oz | ½ cup |
| Lemon essence (teaspoon) | ½/½ | ½ |
| Bicarbonate of soda [baking soda] (teaspoon) | 1/1 | 1 |
| Wooden meat skewers | | |

☐ Measure sugar, syrup, water and glucose into a heavy-gauge saucepan, and heat gently, stirring occasionally until the sugar has completely dissolved.

☐ Increase heat and bring to the boil without stirring. Boil to 148°C [300°F].

☐ Add butter and almonds and boil again until nuts just begin to brown.

☐ Remove pan from heat and sprinkle in the essence and bicarbonate of soda [baking soda].

☐ Stir well allowing the mixture to foam up in the pan.

☐ Arrange wooden meat skewers on an oiled slab.

☐ Using a soup spoon, spoon the mixture over the blunt ends of the skewers.

☐ When cold and set firm, ease the lollipops off the slab, wrap and store in an airtight container.

*These delicious almond brittle lollipops and barley sugar walking sticks are very popular with children. Imagine how thrilled they would be to find them tucked in their lunch box for school and the pleasure they will get in telling their friends 'mummy made them, and why not try one yourself.'*

## Barley sugar walking sticks

These are decorative looking and very popular sweets [candies] particularly enjoyed by children.

| You will need: | Metric/UK | US |
|---|---|---|
| Cubes of lump sugar | 6/6 | 6 |
| Half a lemon | ½/½ | ½ |
| Water | 200ml/7fl oz | ⅞ cup |
| Sugar | 450gm/1 lb | 2⅔ cups |
| Yellow food colouring (drops) | 1–2/1–2 | 1–2 |

☐ Rub sugar cubes on the lemon to absorb full flavour of the zest.
☐ Place cubes, water and sugar in a large, heavy-gauge pan and stir over gentle heat until sugar is dissolved.
☐ Increase heat and bring to the boil, without stirring. Boil to 132°C [270°F].
☐ Remove the pan from heat, stir in colouring, let stand for a few minutes, then pour mixture on to an oiled slab.
☐ When slightly cooled, cut into long strips with an oiled knife.
☐ Use oiled hands to twist and curve the mixture into walking stick shapes.
☐ Allow to become quite cold before wrapping and storing.

## Orange or lemon jellies [Gum-drops]

These are very simple to make and taste fresh and fruity.

| You will need: | Metric/UK | US |
|---|---|---|
| Freshly squeezed lemon or orange juice* | 150ml/5fl oz | ⅝ cup |
| Glycerine | 125ml/4fl oz | ½ cup |
| Gelatine powder | 25gm/1oz | 2 tbsp |
| Castor [fine] sugar | | |

*If orange is used, include a teaspoon or two of lemon juice for tang.
☐ Place the first three ingredients in the top of a double saucepan.
☐ Heat very gently until dissolved, stirring occasionally.
☐ Strain into a jug and then pour on to a plate, or into a sandwich tin or shaped sweet [candy] moulds.
☐ Allow to set for several hours, then cut into cubes with oiled scissors or ease out of the moulds.
☐ Roll the fruit jellies [Gum-drops] in plenty of castor [fine] sugar.
☐ Store in an airtight container in a cool place, and eat fairly soon.

## Date eggs

This, like the other 'egg' sweets [candies] given here, is a very simple recipe and involves no cooking.
Decorate the eggs in any way you choose or copy ideas shown in the photograph.

| You will need: | Metric/UK | US |
|---|---|---|
| Whole dates, stoned | 12/12 | 12 |
| Chopped pistachio nuts | 50gm/2oz | ½ cup |
| Marmalade (tablespoons) | 2/2 | 2 |
| Packet marzipan | 225gm/8oz | |

*Even small children will enjoy making these delightful egg-shaped sweets [candies] that involve no cooking. It is fun deciding how to decorate the egg shapes as well as eating them. So copy some of the designs we have shown you in the photograph and amaze yourself at how simple it is.*

| | Metric/UK | US |
|---|---|---|
| Icing [confectioners'] sugar (tablespoon) | 1/1 | 1 |
| Decorations of your choice | | |

☐ Mix the chopped pistachio nuts and marmalade together in a bowl.
☐ Stuff the dates with the mixture.
☐ Sprinkle the work surface with icing [confectioners'] sugar and roll out the marzipan.
☐ Cut the marzipan into 12 squares.
☐ Roll each date in a marzipan square and mould into an egg shape, then decorate as desired.

## Chocolate eggs

It's a delicious idea to roll these eggs in chocolate sprinkles, coat them with icing [confectioners'] sugar or desiccated [shredded] coconut then decorate with a little melted chocolate.

| You will need: | Metric/UK | US |
|---|---|---|
| Plain sweet biscuits [cookies] | 250gm/9oz | 2¼ cups |
| Cocoa powder (tablespoons) | 2/2 | 2 |
| Ground almonds | 75gm/3oz | ½ cup |

**1.** Humbug [Hard-candy] is worked first with a palette knife and an oiled slab.

**2.** Pull and twist the rope until the mixture is opaque, elastic and shiny.

**3.** Gradually pull it into a long rope shape.

**4.** Use oiled scissors to cut the rope, twisting after each cut is made.

Humbugs [Hard-candies] keep well for two weeks in airtight jars. Use pale coloured soft brown sugar for minty flavoured or dark soft brown sugar for a treacly taste.

| | Metric/UK | US |
|---|---|---|
| Golden [light corn] syrup (tablespoons) | 3/3 | 3 |
| Rum (tablespoons) | 4/4 | 4 |
| Coating and decorations of your choice | | |

☐ Crush the biscuits [cookies] finely, using a rolling pin, and place in a mixing bowl.
☐ Sprinkle with the cocoa powder and ground almonds, and mix together with your hands.
☐ Add the golden [light corn] syrup and rum.
☐ Stir well with a wooden spoon to mix the ingredients thoroughly.
☐ Divide the mixture into 12 pieces and roll into egg shapes with your hands.
☐ Coat and decorate each egg as you wish.

## Apricot eggs
Fun to make (easy enough for children to produce unaided) and delicious to eat.

| You will need: | Metric/UK | US |
|---|---|---|
| Dried apricots | 450gm/1 lb | 2⅔ cups |
| Sugar | 125gm/4oz | ½ cup |
| Marmalade, rounded tablespoon | 1/1 | 1 |
| Packet marzipan | 225gm/8oz | |
| Icing [confectioners'] sugar (tablespoon) | 1/1 | 1 |
| Coating and decorations of your choice | | |

☐ Put the dried apricots twice through a fine mincer [grinder].
☐ Place the minced [ground] apricots in a bowl and mix in the sugar and marmalade.
☐ Using your hands, form the mixture into a roll about 5cm [2in] thick.
☐ Sprinkle the icing [confectioners'] sugar on to the working surface.
☐ Roll the marzipan out into an oblong large enough to wrap round the apricot roll.
☐ Wrap the marzipan round the apricot roll.
☐ Cut the roll into 12 slices and make each slice into an egg shape.
☐ Coat and decorate as you wish.

## Old fashioned humbugs [Hard-candies]
Making humbugs [Hard-candies] requires strong arms. Pulling and twisting the mixture to achieve a smooth, satiny finish may take up to 20 minutes.

| You will need: | Metric/UK | US |
|---|---|---|
| Soft brown sugar | 450gm/1 lb | 2⅔ cups |
| Butter (tablespoons) | 3/3 | 3 |
| Water | 125ml/5fl oz | ⅝ cup |
| Golden [light corn] syrup (tablespoon) | 1/1 | 1 |
| Cream of tartar (teaspoon) | ¼/¼ | ¼ |
| Peppermint oil (drops) | 4/4 | 4 |
| Icing [confectioners'] sugar (tablespoons) | 1–2/1–2 | 1–2 |

☐ Place sugar, butter, water, syrup and cream of tartar in a large heavy-gauge pan and stir over low heat until sugar is completely dissolved.
☐ Increase heat to moderate, cover the pan and cook for 3 minutes.
☐ Uncover the pan and bring the mixture to the boil, without stirring. Boil to 132°C [270°F].
☐ Remove pan from the heat and carefully pour the mixture on to an oiled slab (preferably marble).
☐ Allow to cool for 30 seconds, then sprinkle with the peppermint oil.
☐ Work the mixture with a palette knife until cool enough to handle (fig.1).
☐ Gather up the sugar mixture and twist between well oiled hands to make a rope about 46cm–51cm [18–20in] long.
☐ Fold the rope back on itself and pull and twist again (fig.2). Continue doing this until the mixture is opaque, elastic and shiny.
☐ Wipe the work surface and dust with icing [confectioners'] sugar.
☐ Make the sugar mixture into an egg shape, then flatten the narrow end. Hold the 'egg' in one hand and pull away the narrow end with the other hand to make a long rope about 2cm–2.5cm [¾–1in] thick (fig.3). Let the rope fall in folds on the dusted slab.
☐ Using a pair of well oiled scissors, cut the rope into 2cm–2.5cm [¾–1in] lengths, half twisting the rope after each cut to make the humbugs [Hard-candies] the traditional shape (fig.4).
☐ Cool completely before wrapping and storing in an airtight jar.

## Nougat
Delicious chewy nougat sandwiched between sheets of rice paper – wafer thin, brittle, edible paper which can be bought from good stationers. If you do not own an electric whisk you may need a helping hand with this recipe.

| You will need: | Metric/UK | US |
|---|---|---|
| Rice paper (sheets) | 2–3/2–3 | 2–3 |
| Sugar | 350gm/12oz | 2 cups |
| Water | 150ml/5fl oz | ⅝ cup |
| Liquid glucose | 125gm/4oz | ½ cup |
| Liquid honey | 25gm/1oz | 2 tbsp |
| Large egg white | 1/1 | 1 |
| Cream of tartar (teaspoon) | ⅛/⅛ | ⅛ |
| Halved glacé cherries or other glacé fruit | 50gm/2oz | ½ cup |
| Chopped angelica | 25gm/1oz | 2 tbsp |
| Flaked almonds, chopped brazil or hazel nuts | 25gm/1oz | 2 tbsp |

☐ Damp a 20cm [8in] square sandwich tin and line with rice paper.
☐ Place sugar and water in a heavy pan and stir over very low heat until sugar is completely dissolved.
☐ Add glucose and honey. Increase heat and bring to the boil, without stirring.
☐ Boil to 135°C [275°F].
☐ Meanwhile whisk the egg white with cream of tartar until stiff.

☐ Gradually pour in the hot syrup, whisking all the time.

☐ Continue whisking until the mixture begins to firm, then quickly stir in the fruit and nuts, and tip into the prepared tin. Press down with a metal spoon or spatula.

☐ Cover with a layer of rice paper and leave for at least 12 hours before cutting into bars and wrapping up.

# Marshmallows

These soft, cushion-like sweets [candies] take their name from a plant called the Marsh Mallow, a relative of the hollyhock, which grows in marshy places. They are traditionally pink or white – but there is no reason why your marshmallows should not be flavoured with peppermint and coloured green – or any other original taste and colour scheme you wish!

The delight of marshmallows lies in their versatility for they are delicious served with after-dinner coffee or as everyday treats for the children. Marshmallows are sometimes toasted and often used as decoration for desserts or melted to make a sauce. Children can have great fun toasting marshmallows on an open fire although, of course, adult supervision is essential.

### Marshmallows

Hand-made marshmallows are much more delicious than the bought variety and they are really quite simple to make.

You can roll them in icing [confectioners'] sugar or

**Above:** *Delectable nougat covered with chocolate and others with mixed fruit and nuts.*

**Right:** *Marshmallows whether pink, white or even green, covered in coconut or with a biscuit [cookie] base are delicious to eat.*

desiccated [shredded] coconut, or coat them in melted chocolate.

| You will need: | Metric/UK | US |
|---|---|---|
| Icing [confectioners'] sugar sifted | 125gm/4oz | 1 cup |
| Sugar | 350gm/12oz | 2 cups |
| Powdered glucose (teaspoons) | 2/2 | 2 |
| Water | 275ml/10fl oz | 1¼ cups |
| Gelatine, dissolved in warm water | 25gm/1oz 125ml/4fl oz | ½ cup |
| Egg white beaten until it forms stiff peaks | 1/1 | 1 |
| Vanilla essence (teaspoon) | 1/1 | 1 |

☐ With 25gm/1oz ¼ cup of icing [confectioners'] sugar, lightly dust a 20 x 20cm [8 x 8in] baking tin. Put the remaining icing [confectioners'] sugar on a large plate and set aside.

☐ In a large saucepan, dissolve the sugar and glucose in the water over low heat, stirring constantly. When the sugar has dissolved, increase the heat to moderate and bring the mixture slowly to the boil.

☐ Boil the syrup, without stirring, until the temperature registers 126°C [260°F] on a sugar thermometer or until a little of the syrup dropped into cold water forms a hard ball. Remove the pan from the heat.

☐ Put the dissolved gelatine in a large mixing bowl. Pour the sugar syrup over the gelatine, stirring constantly. Using a wire whisk or rotary beater, beat in the egg white and continue beating until the mixture is stiff. Beat in vanilla essence and spoon mixture into the prepared tin. Set the tin aside to cool.

☐ When cool and set, cut the marshmallow into 2.5cm [1in] squares. Roll the squares in the remaining icing [confectioners'] sugar. Serve or store, well dusted with the icing [confectioners'] sugar, in an airtight tin.

## Marshmallow squares

Marshmallow squares are little biscuit [cookie] squares topped with fruity marshmallow. Children will love them. If you find you have a few left over, they will keep very well in an airtight tin.

| You will need: | Metric/UK | US |
|---|---|---|
| Butter | 175gm/6oz | ¾ cup |
| Sugar | 75gm/3oz | ⅜ cup |
| Vanilla essence (teaspoon) | ½/½ | ½ |
| Flour | 175gm/6oz | 1½ cups |
| Marshmallows | 24/24 | 24 |
| Milk | 75ml/3floz | ⅜ cup |
| Almonds, coarsely chopped | 75gm/3oz | ½ cup |
| Glacé cherries, chopped | 75gm/3oz | ½ cup |

☐ Preheat the oven to warm Gas Mark 3, 170°C [325°F].

☐ In a medium-sized mixing bowl, cream the butter and sugar together with a wooden spoon until the mixture is light and fluffy. Add the vanilla essence and then stir in the flour. Mix well. If the mixture is too dry, add a spoonful of water.

☐ Turn the mixture into a 20 x 20cm [8 x 8in] baking tin. With the back of a spoon, press the mixture down until it is smooth and covers the bottom of the tin.

☐ Place the tin in the oven and bake for 20 to 25 minutes or until the biscuit [cookie] mixture is golden brown. Remove the tin from the oven and set aside to cool.

☐ Meanwhile, in a small heatproof bowl set in a pan of simmering water, melt the marshmallows with the milk over moderate heat, stirring constantly. Remove the pan from the heat and lift out the bowl. Fold in the almonds and cherries. Set the bowl aside to cool slightly, but do not allow the marshmallow mixture to set.

☐ Spoon the marshmallow mixture over the cooled biscuit [cookie] mixture in the baking tin in a thick even layer and set aside until the marshmallow cools and sets.

☐ With a sharp knife, cut the biscuits [cookies] into 5cm [2in] squares and serve immediately or store in an airtight tin.

# Toffee

A perennial favourite with the children and many adults. It is important to use a large saucepan, as the syrup boils up quickly. The temperature given makes a hard, brittle toffee but if you wish to make it softer remove pan from heat after it reaches 155°C[310°F] on a sugar thermometer.

| You will need: | Metric/UK | US |
|---|---|---|
| Vegetable oil (teaspoon) | 1/1 | 1 |
| Soft brown sugar | 350gm/12oz | 2 cups |
| Butter | 75gm/3oz | ⅜ cup |
| Golden [light corn] syrup (tablespoon) | 1/1 | 1 |
| Malt vinegar (teaspoons) | 2/2 | 2 |
| Water (tablespoons) | 3/3 | 3 |

☐ With the oil, grease a 15 x 15cm [6 x 6in] baking tin. Set aside.

☐ In a large saucepan, combine the sugar, butter, syrup, vinegar and water. Place the pan over moderate heat and stir constantly until the sugar has dissolved.

☐ Increase the heat to moderately high and boil the sugar mixture for 10 to 15 minutes or until the temperature reaches 163°C [325°F] on a sugar thermometer, or until a little of the mixture dropped into cold water forms a hard crack. Remove the pan from the heat and allow to cool for 10 minutes.

☐ Pour the toffee into the tin and set aside until it is cool but not set. With an oiled knife cut the toffee into 2.5cm [1in] squares. Leave the toffee until it is completely cold. Remove the toffee from the tin and break it into pieces. Wrap each square of toffee in greaseproof or waxed paper and store in an airtight jar or tin.

## Toffee with almonds and chocolate

This creamy toffee is flavoured with almonds and coated with dark chocolate. These sweets [candies] make ideal presents if they are wrapped in greaseproof or waxed paper and stored in a decorative glass jar.

| You will need: | Metric/UK | US |
|---|---|---|
| Vegetable oil (teaspoon) | 1/1 | 1 |
| Soft brown sugar | 450gm/1 lb | 2⅔ cups |
| Milk | 150ml/5fl oz | ⅝ cup |
| Almond essence (teaspoon) | ½/½ | ½ |
| Flaked almonds | 125gm/4oz | 1 cup |
| Cooking chocolate [semi-sweet], melted and cooled but still liquid | 225gm/8oz | |

☐ With the oil, grease a 15 x 15cm [6 x 6in] baking tin. Set aside.

☐ In a large saucepan, dissolve the sugar in the milk over moderately low heat, stirring constantly. Increase the heat to moderately high and bring the mixture to the boil. Boil the sugar mixture for 10 to 15 minutes or until the temperature reaches 155°C [310°F] on a sugar thermometer or, until a little of the mixture dropped into cold water forms a crack.

☐ Remove the pan from the heat and set aside for 15 minutes. Stir in the almond essence and the flaked almonds. Pour the mixture into the tin and set aside to cool.

☐ When the toffee is cool but not set, cut it into 2.5cm [1in] squares with an oiled knife. Leave the toffee to cool completely.

☐ Remove the squares of toffee from the tin and place them on a wire rack. Place the rack over a clean tray.

☐ Pour teaspoons of the melted chocolate over each toffee to coat it completely. The chocolate which falls on to the tray may be scraped off, melted and re-used.

☐ Set the chocolate-coated toffee aside until they have set completely. Either serve immediately or wrap in waxed paper and store in a cool, dark place.

## Caramels

Hand-made sweets [candies] can be a lot of fun to make and they are, of course, less expensive than the store bought ones. Caramels are among the easiest of all sweets [candies] to make and they may be flavoured as you choose – with chocolate, coffee or maple syrup. For a really professional look, wrap the caramels in waxed paper.

| You will need: | Metric/UK | US |
|---|---|---|
| Butter plus 1 teaspoon butter | 125gm/4oz | ½ cup |
| Soft brown sugar | 225gm/8oz | 1¼ cups |
| Water (tablespoons) | 3/3 | 3 |
| Vanilla essence (teaspoon) | ½/½ | ½ |
| Single [light] cream (tablespoon) | 3/3 | 3 |

☐ Using the teaspoon of butter, lightly grease a large shallow square or rectangular baking pan.

☐ In a medium-sized saucepan, dissolve the brown sugar in the water over moderate heat, stirring constantly with a metal spoon. Add the remaining butter, the vanilla essence and the cream to the pan and boil the mixture, without stirring until it reaches 121°C [250°F] on a sugar thermometer. If you do not have a thermometer, test by removing a teaspoonful of the mixture from the pan and dropping it into a cup of cold water. If the mixture immediately forms a ball, the correct temperature has been reached.

Remove the pan from the heat and pour the caramel into the buttered pan. Set the pan aside to allow the caramel to cool.

When the caramel is cold, use a sharp knife to cut it into squares. Remove the squares from the pan and keep them in an airtight container until you are ready to eat them.

# Brownies

Very popular in the United States and Canada, brownies are inexpensive, moist, chewy little cakes which could not fail to please anyone, whether made with chocolate, marshmallows or nuts.

## Brownies
### Chocolate nut squares
A great American favourite, brownies are nutty chocolate squares. They may be served for tea or with vanilla ice-cream for dessert. They are very easy to make and are best when they are slightly moist and chewy.

| You will need: | Metric/UK | US |
|---|---|---|
| Butter | 125gm/4oz | ½ cup |
| plus 1 teaspoon of butter | | |
| Plain cooking chocolate | 175gm/6oz | |
| Water (tablespoons) | 2/2 | 2 |
| Castor [fine] sugar | 125gm/4oz | ½ cup |
| Vanilla essence (teaspoon) | 1/1 | 1 |
| Self-raising flour | 125gm/4oz | 1 cup |
| Salt (teaspoon) | ⅛/⅛ | ⅛ |
| Eggs | 2/2 | 2 |
| Walnuts, chopped | 50gm/2oz | ⅓ cup |

Preheat the oven to warm Gas Mark 3, 170°C [325°F]. Grease a 20cm [8in] square baking tin with the teaspoon of butter. Set the tin aside.

Put the chocolate, water and butter in a medium-sized

*A great American treat, brownies are delicious to eat for tea, or with ice-cream as a tempting dessert.*

heavy saucepan and melt the chocolate over very low heat, stirring occasionally with a wooden spoon. Remove the pan from the heat and stir in the sugar and vanilla. Set the pan aside and allow the chocolate mixture to cool to room temperature.

Sift the flour and salt into a medium-sized mixing bowl. Gradually stir in the cooled chocolate mixture. Add the eggs and beat well. Fold in the walnuts. Pour the mixture into the buttered tin.

Bake in the oven for 30 to 35 minutes or until a knife plunged into the centre of the cake comes out clean. When the cake is cool cut it into squares.

## Butterscotch brownies
### Nutty butterscotch cakes
Simple to make, butterscotch brownies are equally popular with children and adults.

| You will need: | Metric/UK | US |
|---|---|---|
| Butter (teaspoon) | 1/1 | 1 |
| Butter, melted | 125gm/4oz | ½ cup |
| Brown sugar | 175gm/6oz | 1 cup |
| Eggs | 2/2 | 2 |
| Salt (teaspoon) | ⅛/⅛ | ⅛ |
| Self-raising flour | 125gm/4oz | 1 cup |
| Vanilla essence (teaspoon) | 1/1 | 1 |
| Walnuts, coarsely chopped | 50gm/2oz | ⅓ cup |

Preheat the oven to moderate heat, Gas Mark 4, 180°C [350°F]. Grease a 20cm [8in] baking tin with the 1 teaspoon of butter.

Put all the remaining ingredients in a large mixing bowl and thoroughly mix them together with a wooden spoon. Pour the mixture into the greased baking tin.

Bake in the oven for 25 minutes, or until the top is firm. Cut into squares while warm. Cool to room temperature before serving.

**Left:** *Very popular in the United States and Canada, mallow brownies are inexpensive, moist cakes that taste delicious.*
**Right:** *Fudge and nougat are delightful nut-studded sweets [candies] that go particularly well with after-dinner coffee though you will find it difficult to stop yourself eating them straight away.*

thoroughly combined. Stir in the walnuts.

☐ Spoon the mixture into the prepared tin, smoothing the top with a flat-bladed knife. Place the tin in the centre of the oven and bake for 30 minutes. Remove the tin from the oven and set aside.

☐ Place the marshmallows in a small saucepan. Set the pan over moderate heat and melt the marshmallows, stirring constantly. Remove the pan from the heat. Pour the melted marshmallows over the top of the cake.

☐ Place the remaining butter, sugar, salt and the cream in a small saucepan. Place the pan over high heat and bring the mixture to the boil. Continue boiling until the temperature reaches 115°C [240°F] on a sugar thermometer (soft ball stage).

☐ Remove the pan from the heat and allow the mixture to cool, without stirring, for 4 minutes. Beat in the remaining vanilla essence. Continue beating until the syrup is thick and creamy.

☐ Pour the mixture evenly over the marshmallow topping. Allow the cake to cool completely in the tin before cutting it into squares.

# Fudge

This is a creamy, chocolate-flavoured fudge which is easy to make. Chopped almonds or hazelnuts may be stirred into the fudge mixture, as an alternative.

| You will need: | Metric/UK | US |
|---|---|---|
| Butter | 50gm/2oz | $\frac{1}{4}$ cup |
| plus 1 teaspoon of butter | | |
| Sugar | 450gm/1 lb | 2$\frac{2}{3}$ cups |
| Milk | 150ml/5 fl oz | $\frac{5}{8}$ cup |
| Dark [semi-sweet] cooking chocolate, broken into small pieces | 50gm/2oz | |

☐ Using the teaspoon of butter, grease a 20 x 20cm [8 x 8in] square cake tin and set it aside.

☐ In a medium-sized, heavy saucepan, combine the sugar, milk and chocolate. Place the pan over moderate heat and stir until the sugar and chocolate have dissolved.

☐ Increase the heat to high and boil, without stirring (unless the mixture shows signs of burning), until the mixture registers 115°C [240°F] on a sugar thermometer, or until a little of the fudge dropped into cold water forms a soft ball. Remove the pan from the heat and set aside for 5 minutes.

☐ Cut the remaining butter into small pieces. When the fudge mixture has cooled slightly, beat in the butter. Beat until the butter has melted and the mixture is thick and smooth.

☐ Pour the fudge into the prepared tin and allow it to cool and harden slightly before making it into squares.

## Mallow brownies

Mallow brownies are popularly known as "snackin" cakes, and should be cut into small squares as they are very sweet.

| You will need: | Metric/UK | US |
|---|---|---|
| Butter, melted | 150gm/5oz | $\frac{5}{8}$ cup |
| plus 1 teaspoon of butter | | |
| Flour | 75gm/3oz | $\frac{3}{4}$ cup |
| plus 1 tablespoon of flour | | |
| Baking powder (teaspoon) | 1/1 | 1 |
| Salt (teaspoon) | $\frac{1}{2}$/$\frac{1}{2}$ | $\frac{1}{2}$ |
| Soft brown sugar | 425gm/15oz | 2$\frac{1}{2}$ cups |
| Lightly beaten egg yolks | 2/2 | 2 |
| Vanilla essence (teaspoons) | 2/2 | 2 |
| Walnuts, chopped | 75gm/3oz | $\frac{1}{2}$ cup |
| Large marshmallows | 20/20 | 20 |
| Single [light] cream | 75ml/3 fl oz | $\frac{3}{8}$ cup |

☐ Preheat the oven to moderate, Gas Mark 4, 180°C [350°F].

☐ With the teaspoon of butter, grease a 20cm [8in] square cake tin. Sprinkle with the tablespoon of flour and knock out any excess.

☐ Sift the remaining flour, the baking powder and half the salt into a small mixing bowl. Set aside.

☐ In a medium-sized mixing bowl, combine 175gm/6oz 1 cup of the sugar, the egg yolks and 1 teaspoon of the vanilla essence with 75gm/3oz $\frac{3}{4}$ cup of the remaining butter, beating until the ingredients are well blended. With a metal spoon, fold the flour mixture into the sugar and butter mixture. Mix well until all the ingredients are

## Fudge II

This delicious rich fudge is flavoured with vanilla and has a softer, smoother texture than the chocolate fudge. For a lighter-coloured fudge, substitute white sugar for brown.

| You will need: | Metric/UK | US |
|---|---|---|
| Butter<br>plus 1 teaspoon of butter | 50gm/2oz | ¼ cup |
| Evaporated milk | 225ml/8fl oz | 1 cup |
| Water | 50ml/2fl oz | ¼ cup |
| Light brown sugar | 450gm/1 lb | 2⅔ cups |
| Vanilla essence (teaspoon) | ½/½ | ½ |

☐ Using the teaspoon of butter, grease a 20 x 20cm [8 x 8in] square baking tin, and set it aside.

☐ In a medium-sized heavy saucepan, combine the milk, water and sugar. Place the pan over low heat and stir until the sugar has dissolved. Cut the remaining butter into small pieces and add it to the mixture. Cook, stirring constantly, until it has melted.

☐ Increase the heat to high and boil the mixture, stirring occasionally, until it registers 115°C [240°F] on a sugar thermometer, or until a little of the fudge dropped into cold water forms a soft ball. Reduce the heat to moderate. Stir in the vanilla essence. Cook, stirring constantly, until the mixture is smooth and thick and begins to form grains, rather like semolina. Remove the pan from the heat.

☐ Pour the mixture into the prepared tin. Leave the fudge until it is cold and cut it into 2.5cm [1in] squares. Chill in the refrigerator before removing from the tin and serving.

## Fudge fingers

These superb nutty chocolate-flavoured fingers are very easy and quick to make.

| You will need: | Metric/UK | US |
|---|---|---|
| Butter<br>plus 1 teaspoon of butter | 125gm/4oz | ½ cup |
| Soft brown sugar | 175gm/6oz | 1 cup |
| Double [heavy] cream | 50ml/2fl oz | ¼ cup |
| Dark [semi-sweet] cooking chocolate | 50gm/2oz | |
| Walnuts, chopped | 125gm/4oz | ⅔ cup |
| Blanched hazelnuts, lightly toasted and chopped | 50gm/2oz | ⅓ cup |
| Digestive biscuits [graham crackers], crushed | 225gm/8oz | |

☐ Grease a shallow 28 x 18cm [11 x 7in] baking tin, with the teaspoon of butter. Set aside.

☐ In a medium-sized, heavy saucepan, combine the sugar, remaining butter, cream and chocolate. Place the pan over moderate heat and cook, stirring constantly, until the sugar has dissolved and the chocolate has melted.

☐ Remove the pan from the heat. Stir in the nuts and crushed biscuits [crackers] and combine well.

☐ Turn the mixture into the prepared tin and press it down with a flat-bladed knife.

☐ Place the tin in the refrigerator and chill for at least 1 hour before cutting into finger shapes and serving to your guests.

**Above:** *Hand-made date fudge is so simple yet different to make. It will keep for several weeks in an airtight container.*
**Right:** *Easy-to-make peppermint creams may be cut into many different decorative shapes and coloured in many exciting ways – pink, green or even yellow! You could try your hand at making them look like a chequer board of many different colours. Delight your friends with your originality and make them today.*

## Date fudge

There are few sweets [candies] quite so delicious as hand-made fudge. Date fudge is very easy to make and will keep for several weeks in an airtight tin. It is best to use a sugar thermometer, but if you do not have one, test the fudge mixture by dropping a teaspoonful into cold water. If it forms a soft ball, the correct temperature has been reached.

| You will need: | Metric/UK | US |
|---|---|---|
| Butter<br>plus 1 teaspoon of butter | 125gm/4oz | ½ cup |
| Sugar | 450gm/1 lb | 2⅔ cups |
| Water | 150ml/5fl oz | ⅝ cup |
| Dates, stoned and finely chopped | 125gm/4oz | ⅔ cup |
| Clear honey (tablespoons) | 4/4 | 4 |

☐ Using the teaspoon of butter, lightly grease a shallow 20cm [8in] square tin and set it aside.

☐ Place the remaining butter, sugar, water, dates and honey in a medium-sized saucepan. Place the pan over low heat. With a wooden spoon, stir the mixture until the sugar is dissolved. Increase the heat to moderate. Bring the mixture slowly to the boil. Boil until the fudge reaches 115°C [240°F] on a sugar thermometer (the soft ball stage).

☐ Remove the pan from the heat. With a wooden spoon, beat the mixture until it is the consistency of thick cream.

☐ Pour the mixture into the tin. With a sharp knife mark the fudge into 2.5cm [1in] squares. Leave until it is completely cold.

☐ Cut the fudge into pieces when it is cold and store it in an airtight tin.

## Peppermint creams

These inexpensive and easy-to-make sweets [candies] will give children great pleasure to make to impress their family and friends for a special treat or gift. They are also the perfect accompaniment to after-dinner coffee. If a very strong peppermint taste is desired, the amount of peppermint essence may be increased. The shape of the sweets [candies] may also be varied by using heart-shaped or diamond-shaped pastry cutters. If stored in an air tight tin or container these attractive sweets [candies] will keep for up to two weeks.

| You will need: | Metric/UK | US |
| --- | --- | --- |
| Icing [confectioners'] sugar sifted | 450gm/1 lb | 4 cups |
| Lemon juice (teaspoon) | 1/1 | 1 |
| Egg white | 1/1 | 1 |
| Peppermint essence (drops) | 4/4 | 4 |

☐ In a large mixing bowl, combine all of the ingredients together with a wooden spoon, beating until they are well mixed.

☐ Generously sprinkle a large board or slab with icing [confectioners'] sugar and turn the peppermint mixture out on to it. Using a rolling pin sprinkled with icing [confectioners'] sugar, roll out the mixture to 6mm [¼in] thick. Using 1.3cm [½in] round pastry cutter, cut the mixture into circles or any other shape you require.

## Fig and nut sweets [candies]

Because they contain no added sugar, these attractive little Portuguese sweets [candies] are much better for children's teeth. They also make a deliciously different after-dinner treat served with coffee or a liqueur.

| You will need: | Metric/UK | US |
| --- | --- | --- |
| Dried figs, stalks removed and coarsely chopped | 350gm/12oz | 2 cups |
| Dates, stoned and finely chopped | 125gm/4oz | ⅔ cup |
| Whole blanched almonds, toasted | 30/30 | 30 |
| Hazelnuts, finely chopped | 65gm/2½oz | ½ cup |
| Blanched almonds, finely chopped | 65gm/2½oz | ½ cup |

☐ Using a food mill, purée the chopped figs and dates into a medium-sized mixing bowl. Alternatively, purée them in a blender and transfer tham to a bowl.

☐ With your hands, shape the fruit mixture into 30 small balls. Push the whole almond into the centre of each ball, making sure the almond is completely covered.

☐ Spread out the chopped hazelnuts and almonds on a sheet of greaseproof or waxed paper. Roll each ball in the nuts so that it is completely covered.

☐ Pile the sweets [candies] on an attractive serving plate. Sprinkle over any remaining chopped nuts and serve.

# Fun to make sweet to eat

## Toffee apples

Family favourites, toffee apples are enjoyed by all ages – young as well as old. For adults they revive nostalgic memories of Hallowe'en, Guy Fawkes and 4th July when sticky fingers from toffee apples were just as enjoyable as all the other attractions. For children they are a treat that cannot be missed. More sophisticated palates will appreciate the exotic flavour of toffee apples Chinese-style which makes a delightfully unusual after-dinner dessert.

### Toffee apples

If you can't get your children to eat apples, they will if you serve them this way! The brittle toffee contrasts so well with apples.

| You will need: | Metric/UK | US |
|---|---|---|
| Green eating apples | 10/10 | 10 |
| Wooden sticks | 10/10 | 10 |
| **Toffee** | | |
| Soft brown sugar | 450gm/1 lb | 2⅔ cups |
| Butter | 50gm/2oz | ¼ cup |
| Malt vinegar (teaspoons) | 2/2 | 2 |
| Water | 150ml/5fl oz | ⅝ cup |
| Golden [light corn] syrup (tablespoons) | 2/2 | 2 |

☐ First prepare the toffee. In a large saucepan, combine the sugar, butter, vinegar, water and syrup.

☐ Place the pan over moderately low heat and, stirring constantly, cook the mixture until the sugar has dissolved and the butter melted. Increase the heat to moderately high and boil the mixture for 10 to 15 minutes or until the temperature reaches 163°C [325°F] on a sugar thermometer or, until a little of the mixture dropped into cold water forms a hard crack.

☐ Remove the pan from the heat.

☐ After thoroughly washing the apples, spear them with the sticks and, tipping the pan, dip the apples in the toffee. Place the apples, stick end uppermost, on lightly oiled greaseproof or waxed paper.

☐ Set the toffee apples aside to cool completely. Either serve the apples immediately or wrap them in greaseproof paper and store in an airtight tin.

## Toffee apples Chinese-style

This sophisticated version of toffee apples requires a little time and patience during the preparation, but it makes an ideal dessert for a Chinese meal and special occasions.

| You will need: | Metric/UK | US |
|---|---|---|
| Bananas, peeled, halved lengthways and cut into 2.5cm [1in] lengths | 3/3 | 3 |
| Apples, peeled, cored and cut into 8 slices | 2/2 | 2 |
| 1 tablespoon lemon juice mixed with 1 tablespoon water | | |
| Peanut oil (tablespoon) | 1/1 | 1 |
| Sugar | 225gm/8oz | 1 cup |
| Water | 50ml/2fl oz | ¼ cup |
| Sesame seeds (tablespoons) | 2/2 | 2 |
| Sufficient vegetable oil for deep-frying | | |
| **Batter** | | |
| Flour | 50gm/2oz | ½ cup |
| Egg lightly beaten | 1/1 | 1 |
| Milk | 125ml/4fl oz | ½ cup |

☐ Place the bananas and the apples in a medium-sized mixing bowl and pour over the lemon juice mixture, stirring until the fruit is well coated with the liquid. Set aside.

☐ To make the batter, sift the flour into a medium-sized mixing bowl. Make a well in the centre and pour in the beaten egg and half the milk. Using a wooden spoon, gradually draw the flour into the liquid. Beat the batter until it is smooth and thick. Stir in the remaining milk. Set aside.

☐ In a medium-sized saucepan, combine the peanut oil, sugar, water and sesame seeds. Place the pan over moderate heat and cook, stirring constantly, until the sugar has dissolved. Increase the heat to moderately high and boil the mixture for 10 minutes or until it is light golden in colour. Remove the pan from the heat. Set aside.

☐ With a slotted spoon, remove the bananas and apples

*Toffee apples are everybody's favourites usually associated with special occasions. Don't wait for Halloween, or the 4th of July make them today as a real treat for the family.*

from the bowl and drain them on kitchen paper towels.

☐ Fill a deep-drying pan one-third full with the vegetable oil and heat the oil over moderate heat until it reaches 175°C [375°F] on a deep-fat thermometer or until a cube of stale bread dropped into the oil turns golden brown in 40 seconds.

☐ Dip the bananas and apples in the batter and place them into the oil, a few at a time. Fry for 2 minutes or until the batter is puffed up and golden brown. With a slotted spoon, remove the fruit from the pan and allow to drain on kitchen paper towels. Keep warm while you fry the remaining fruit.

☐ Return the saucepan containing the sesame seed mixture to moderately high heat and boil for a further 5 minutes or until the syrup is golden brown in colour. Remove the pan from the heat.

☐ Lift the pieces of fruit with a pair of chopsticks or two forks and dip them into the syrup, coating them thoroughly and draining off any excess. Arrange the fruit on a lightly oiled serving dish and serve immediately.

# Marzipan animals

The exact origins of marzipan are obscure. Some say that it was introduced to Europe by the Arabs, and some that it was created by an ancient order of nuns in France. Whatever the beginnings, this sweetmeat is now popular throughout the world – as a covering for cakes, for *petits fours*, and for moulding into delightful miniature animals and fruit.

Marzipan (or marchpane or almond paste as it is variously called) is a mixture of pounded almonds and sugars bound together with eggs and flavourings. It can be made with or without cooking. Either method will produce a pale-coloured marzipan into which vegetable-based food dyes can be kneaded to create fresh, delicate colours. The cooked method, which involves a hot sugar syrup, produces a superior marzipan – smooth textured and ideal for intricate moulding.

Marzipan bought in packets from grocers and supermarkets is usually made by the boiled syrup method. It is therefore fine enough for intricate moulding. It is convenient when you are pressed for time but its distinctive yellow colouring is somewhat restricting.

### Boiled marzipan

This recipe can be used for moulding intricate shapes as well as *petits fours* and simple shapes. The marzipan remains excellent to eat for two months, although it will begin to go hard on the outside and to look a little dusty.

| You will need: | Metric/UK | US |
|---|---|---|
| Sugar | 450gm/1 lb | 2⅔ cups |
| Water | 200ml/7fl oz | ⅞ cup |
| Ground almonds | 350gm/12oz | 1½ cups |
| Egg whites, lightly beaten | 2/2 | 2 |
| Orange flower water (teaspoon) | 1/1 | 1 |
| Lemon juice (tablespoons) | 2/2 | 2 |
| Icing [confectioners'] sugar (tablespoons) | 4/4 | 4 |

[9 x 12in], with greased greaseproof paper.

☐ Put the butter or margarine, sugar, treacle and syrup in a pan. Place over gentle heat and stir till butter melts.

☐ Remove from heat, add milk and set aside to cool a little.

☐ Lightly whisk the eggs.

☐ Sift all remaining ingredients into mixing bowl.

☐ Stir in syrup mixture, then the beaten eggs.

☐ Pour the mixture into prepared tin and bake just above the centre of the oven for 50–60 minutes till golden and firm to touch.

☐ Leave in tin for 5 minutes, then turn out on to cooling tray and remove paper.

## Decorating a bunny cake

| You will need: | Metric/UK | US |
| --- | --- | --- |
| A piece of card or paper | | |
| 2 or 3 cocktail sticks | | |
| Icing [confectioners'] sugar (tablespoon) | 1/1 | 1 |
| **Butter icing** | | |
| Butter or margarine creamed with | 25gm/1oz | 2 tbsp |
| Icing [confectioners'] sugar sifted | 50gm/2oz | ½ cup |
| Packet sugar-coated chocolate drops | 1/1 | 1 |

☐ Place cake on a board. If the top surface is not flat turn cake upside down.

☐ Cut a piece of paper to size of cooked cake. Draw a bunny shape on the piece of paper and cut it out.

☐ Place the bunny shape on top of cake and secure with cocktail sticks.

☐ Put a tablespoon of icing [confectioners'] sugar in a

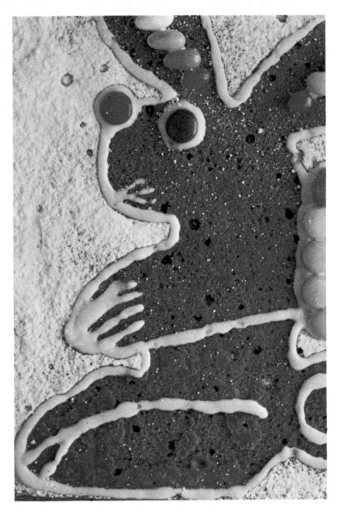

**Above:** *A gingerbread bunny cake is a real novelty.*
**Below:** *Other shapes you can make with your gingerbread that will amuse children for many happy hours.*

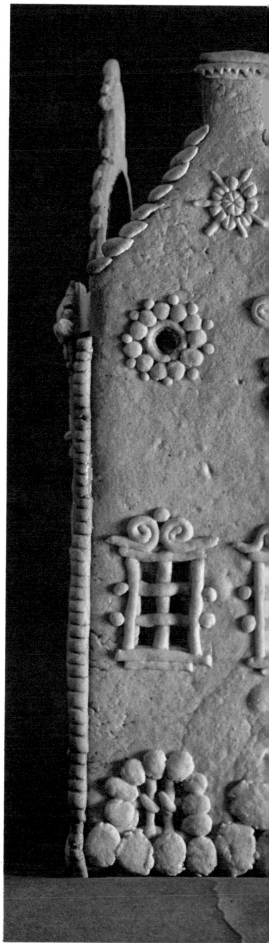

24

sieve and sift sugar over the uncovered cake.

☐ Carefully remove cocktail sticks and lift off the paper. The bunny shape is now neatly outlined in sugar.

☐ If desired, the bunny shape can be piped in with the butter icing using a forcing bag and plain icing tube.

☐ Arrange chocolate drops on the bunny to represent ears, eyes and pack. 'Glue' them with butter icing.

## Making gingerbread houses and figures

Most children know the story of Hansel and Gretel, and love gingerbread boys and girls. The traditional gingerbread biscuit [cookies] recipe given here is easy to make, so children can enjoy assembling and mixing the ingredients with adult supervision. Then there is the fun of deciding on shapes to be cut.

Always keep outline biscuit [cookie] shapes quite simple as it can be difficult to cut round complicated shapes. Draw the shapes on card, cut out neatly and use as a template to cut the dough. A round-bladed knife is best as it cuts dough without tearing.

Gingerbread boys and girls are simply shaped (fig.1) but, once the biscuits [cookies] are cooked, there is a splendid opportunity for even very small children to indulge in fantasy decorations to complete the edible works of art. Coloured icing, candied peel, hundreds and thousands, currants, nuts, chocolate drops, silver balls and all sorts of sweets [candies] can be used. Nimble fingered cooks can make more elaborate biscuits [cookies]. This gingerbread dough is firm enough to make surface decorations – so you can roll tiny balls and strips of dough and superimpose them on top of the basic cut-out biscuit [cookie] shapes before cooking. Have fun adding facial expressions and clothes to figures, or decorating walls with ornate window and door frames, rambling roses or what you will. And once cooked, four biscuit [cookie] walls can be 'glued' to cardboard with a little icing to make a 3-dimensional building.

## Traditional gingerbread biscuit [cookie]

| You will need: | Metric/UK | US |
|---|---|---|
| Egg | 1/1 | 1 |
| Black treacle [molasses] (tablespoon) | 1/1 | 1 |
| Castor [fine] sugar | 200gm/7oz | $\frac{7}{8}$ cup |
| Ground cinnamon (teaspoons) | 2/2 | 2 |
| Ground cardamom (teaspoons) | 2/2 | 2 |
| Ground mace (teaspoon) | $\frac{1}{2}/\frac{1}{2}$ | $\frac{1}{2}$ |
| Butter or margarine | 250gm/9oz | 1 cup |
| Baking powder (teaspoons) | $1\frac{1}{2}/1\frac{1}{2}$ | $1\frac{1}{2}$ |
| Plain flour | 300gm/11oz | $1\frac{1}{2}$ cups |

☐ Place egg, treacle [molasses], sugar and spices in a bowl and beat well together.

☐ Melt butter or margarine and, when it begins to cool, blend into mixture.

☐ Sift baking powder and flour together, add to mixture and bind well using your hands.

☐ Wrap the dough in aluminium foil and chill for 30 minutes.

☐ Heat over to Gas Mark 3, 170°C [325°F] and grease several baking trays.

☐ Roll dough out on a lightly floured surface, making it

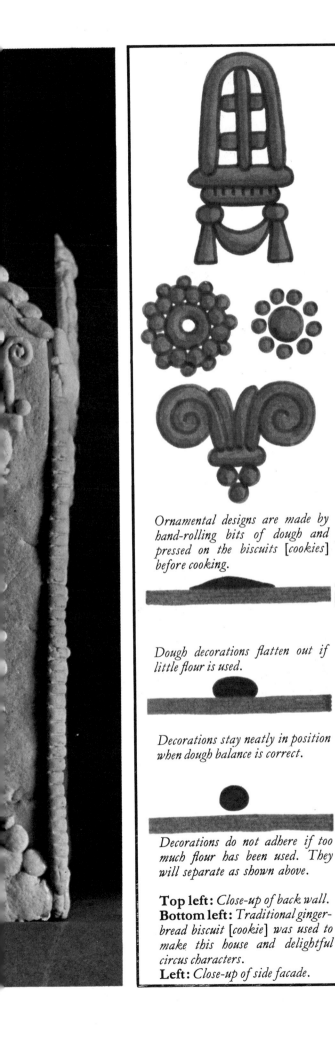

*Ornamental designs are made by hand-rolling bits of dough and pressed on the biscuits [cookies] before cooking.*

*Dough decorations flatten out if little flour is used.*

*Decorations stay neatly in position when dough balance is correct.*

*Decorations do not adhere if too much flour has been used. They will separate as shown above.*

**Top left:** *Close-up of back wall.*
**Bottom left:** *Traditional gingerbread biscuit [cookie] was used to make this house and delightful circus characters.*
**Left:** *Close-up of side facade.*

slightly thicker than usual for biscuits [cookies].

☐ Cut into shapes required and place on baking trays. Simple gingerbread boys and girls can all be cooked straight away.

☐ But if the biscuits [cookies] are to have surface dough decorations now is the time to add them. Use your hands to roll little bits of dough into strips and small balls. Press the decorations firmly into the uncooked biscuits [cookies] using the back of a knife, so that the decorations are partially embedded, not simply lying on top of the biscuits [cookies].

☐ Test bake a few decorated biscuits [cookies] first to check your dough is of a correct consistency. Flours vary and a little more may be needed of one type than another.

fig. 1

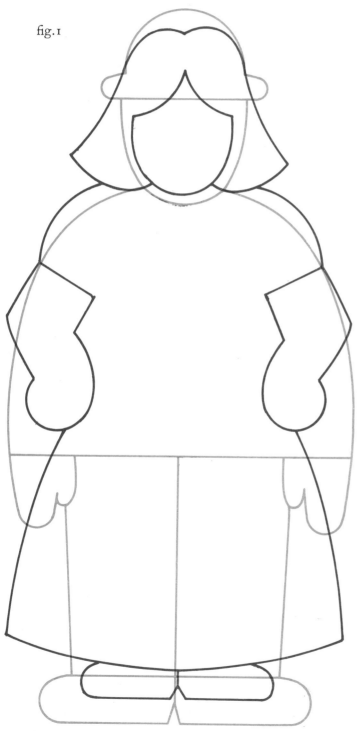

**Above:** *Traditionally, gingerbread figures were decorated with wafers of edible gold leaf, but without they still look festive.*
**Left:** *Trace patterns: gingerbread boy (blue) and girl (pink).*

If too much flour has been used the decorations will not adhere to the biscuit [cookie] during cooking. If too little has been used the decoration will flatten out (fig 2).

☐ Bake one tray first for 15–20 minutes till lightly brown.

☐ Leave for 5 minutes on tray, then transfer to wire rack to cool (if the walls of a house have bulged during cooking, trim them straight with a set square and sharp knife as soon as the biscuits [cookies] are removed from the oven).

☐ Check that the biscuit [cookie] decoration is the correct consistency – if necessary knead a little more flour or two teaspoons of beaten egg into the remaining biscuit [cookie] dough before decorating and baking the remaining biscuits [cookies].

# A log cabin

Can you imagine a more mouth-watering centrepiece for a children's party than this gaily-coloured log cabin made with all their favourite goodies-sweets [candies] growing in the garden and biscuits [cookies] covering the roof. It's great fun to make and even better to eat! It measures about 20.5cm [8in] long by 10cm [4in] wide by 12.5cm [5in] high.

| You will need: | Metric/UK | US |
|---|---|---|
| Ginger slab cakes | 3/3 | 3 |
| Assortment of coloured sweets [candies] like dolly mixtures, jelly beans, liquorice allsorts and comfits, fudge, chocolate drops, toasted coconut sweets [candies], jelly drops, marzipan fruits | | |
| Lollipops | 2/2 | 2 |
| Plain rectangular biscuits [cookies] | | |
| Chocolate rectangular biscuits [cookies] | | |
| Chocolate fingers | | |
| Icing [confectioners'] sugar | | |
| Scrap of aluminium foil for pond | | |
| Toothpicks | 2/2 | 2 |
| Stiff cardboard 30.5 x 38cm [12 x 15in] for base | | |

## Making the basic log cabin
☐ The basic log cabin shape consists of two gingerbread cakes for the walls and one for the roof. Place the two wall cakes, on their long sides, centrally on the base joining them with toothpicks (be sure to remove these when the cake is cut). Cut the third cake diagonally with a bread knife as shown in the diagram and place it on top of the walls.

## Decorating the walls
☐ Use a stiff mixture of icing [confectioners'] sugar and water to stick the sweets [candies] and biscuits [cookies] to the log cabin.
☐ The roof is covered by plain biscuits [cookies] with a fudge chimney and a jelly bean ridge. The door is a chocolate biscuit [cookie]; the windows are pieces of fudge surrounded by liquorice comfits. Chocolate fingers are placed at the corners of the walls.
☐ Cover the rest of the side, back and front walls as you please, using lots of brightly-coloured sweets [candies].

## Decorating the garden
☐ Surround the log cabin with a wall of toasted coconut sweets [candies] and jelly drops. The gate is made of liquorice logs and comfits, and the crazy paving path is cut-up fudge.
☐ Make a pond from the aluminium foil and a log pile

*See how your children's faces will light up when you present them with this log cabin packed full of their favourite goodies. It involves no cooking just endless hours of creative fun.*

from liquorice logs. Use green sweets [candies] for the grass, cutting them in half if necessary. Add coloured sweets [candies] and marzipan fruits for the flowers and fruit in the garden. The trees are lollipops stuck into a jelly drop base.
☐ Finally, cover the remaining cardboard base with coloured paper, crackers, more sweets [candies] or little cakes.

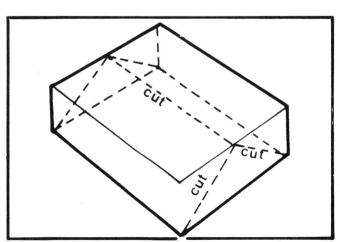

# Icing cookies is child's play

It's fun to make mud pies, build sand castles and mould fantastic shapes in plasticine – but the results make disappointing if not disastrous eating.

Real cookies are far more rewarding. Children can use their creative skills and enjoy a delicious tea-time treat at the end of the afternoon.

Happy hours can be spent designing biscuit [cookie] shapes and, once the biscuits [cookies] are cooked, there is the joy of icing and decorating. Even adults will find these ideas fun and may want to try them on a somewhat more elevated level, in order to make entertaining presents for children.

The shortcake biscuit [cookie] recipe given here is simple enough for children to prepare unaided. Small children must not, of course, be allowed to touch the oven; an adult should place the baking tray in the oven and remove it when the biscuits [cookies] are cooked.

The dough is easily handled but, if it becomes too soft, it can be wrapped in foil and chilled in the refrigerator for 20–30 minutes. Afternatively, knead in a little extra flour – up to 25gm [1oz].

## Making picture shapes

Children will find it fascinating to turn their own painted pictures into edible works of art.

It's exciting to create special pictures of animals, people, ships, trains or buildings, then cut the traced outline shapes in dough with a rounded knife blade.

It's fun, too, to 'paint' the cooked pictures with lots of icing and other delicious decorations.

It's also fun to put your hand on the dough, trace round it with a cutting wheel, and bake your 'hand'. Then decorate it with an icing watch, bracelet or rings. You could use split blanched almonds for finger nails, perhaps dipped in a little melted chocolate for anyone whose finger nails are not always that clean!

## Delicious decorations

If the dough is simply rolled into balls between the hands, or if shaped biscuit [cookie] cutters are used, the children's main pleasure will be concentrated on decorating the cooked biscuits [cookies], so a generous supply of materials will be needed. A popular selection might include blanched whole nuts, chopped nuts, candied peel, currants, chocolate sprinkles, multi-coloured hundreds and thousands, sugar-coated flowers, silver balls, desic-cated [shredded] coconut, icing [confectioners'] sugar, glacé cherries, sugar-coated chocolate drops, glacé icing and butter icing.

After you have finished decorating the many different biscuit [cookie] shapes you will have made – not only will you get great pleasure in eating them yourself but think how thrilled your family and friends will be to receive such a delightful and original gift so delicious to eat!

## Shortcake biscuits [cookies]

| You will need: | Metric/UK | US |
|---|---|---|
| Soft margarine | 125gm/4oz | ½ cup |
| Butter | 75gm/3oz | ⅜ cup |
| Sifted [confectioners'] sugar | 50gm/2oz | ½ cup |
| Sifted plain flour | 150gm/5oz | 1¼ cups |
| Sifted self-raising flour | 125gm/4oz | 1¼ cups |
| Cornflour [cornstarch] (tablespoon) | 1/1 | 1 |

☐ Place margarine and butter in a bowl and beat well.
☐ Gradually add the icing [confectioners'] sugar and continue beating the mixture till light and fluffy.
☐ Then work in the two sifted flours and cornflour [cornstarch]. Knead lightly to make a smooth dough.
☐ Wrap the dough in tin foil and chill for 30 minutes.
☐ Heat the oven to Gas Mark 4, 180°C [350°F].
☐ Lightly flour the pastry board and roll out dough to 6mm [¼in] thick.
☐ Cut out biscuits [cookies], place on baking trays and cook for 15 minutes or until light brown.
☐ Cool for one minute then transfer to a wire rack. Decorate when cold.

## Butter icing

| You will need: | Metric/UK | US |
|---|---|---|
| Butter | 50gm/2oz | ¼ cup |
| Sifted icing [confectioners'] sugar | 125gm/4oz | 1 cup |
| Vanilla essence (drops) | 2/2 | 2 |
| Milk (tablespoon) | 1/1 | 1 |

☐ Cream the butter lightly.
☐ Beat in the icing [confectioners'] sugar a little at a time. Continue beating till really light and fluffy.
☐ Then beat in the vanilla and milk.

## Glacé icing

| You will need: | Metric/UK | US |
|---|---|---|
| Sifted icing [confectioners'] sugar | 50gm/2oz | ½ cup |
| Lemon juice or warm water (tablespoon) | ½–1/½–1 | ½–1 |

☐ Put the icing [confectioners'] sugar in a bowl and add half a tablespoon of liquid.
☐ Beat well with a wooden spoon.
☐ If the icing is smooth and of a consistency that will coat the back of the spoon no more liquid is needed. If not, add more liquid to get the right consistency.

*Children will spend many happy hours making and decorating these easy-to-make bunny shapes that are attractive as well as delicious to eat. Multi-coloured hundreds and thousands, chocolate sprinkles, silver balls, sugar-coated chocolate drops, glacé icing, cherries and nuts are just a few ideas for decorating your bunny biscuits [cookies]. No doubt you will be able to think of many more delicious and inviting finishing touches.*

# Bunny biscuits

1. Lightly knead the shortcake biscuit [cookie] mixture to make a smooth dough, wrap it up in aluminium foil and chill in the refrigerator for 30 minutes.

2. Meanwhile paint your pictures. It saves a great deal of time if you paint them on tracing paper. Try ideas like bunnies, tortoises or houses. Keep shapes bold.

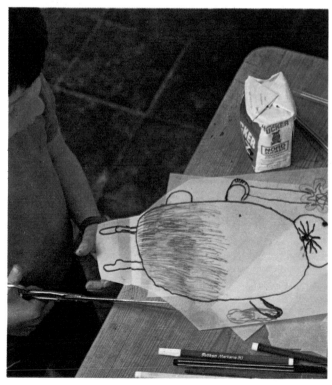

3. Make things like rabbit's ears and legs quite big because thin bits of biscuit [cookie] may get broken off.

4. Using scissors, cut out your pictures. Cut the rough shape first, then around the actual outlines you have drawn.

**5.** *Place the tracing paper cut out on the chilled and rolled out dough. Use one hand to hold the paper firmly in position while you cut round it with a knife.*

**6.** *A round-bladed knife will cut the dough without tearing it and make the edges precise. While the biscuits [cookies] cook, prepare some glacé and butter icing (recipes are given).*

**7.** *When the cooked biscuits [cookies] are cold, begin to decorate them. Use sweets [candies] and nuts as well as icing.*

**8.** *Completed bunny biscuits [cookies] look almost too good to eat but they are sure to taste too delicious to resist.*

31

# Ornamental painted biscuits

What can be more delightful than to combine your skills as a cook with your creative talents as an artist. Few culinary projects offer more scope to do this than these enchanting painted biscuits [cookies]. They can be special gifts in themselves or stocking fillers at Christmas or prizes for a kiddies party. Why not give one to your favourite person on Valentine's day. The only danger is that they will look so good you won't want to eat them!

*These traditional German biscuits [cookies] were made with special moulds.*

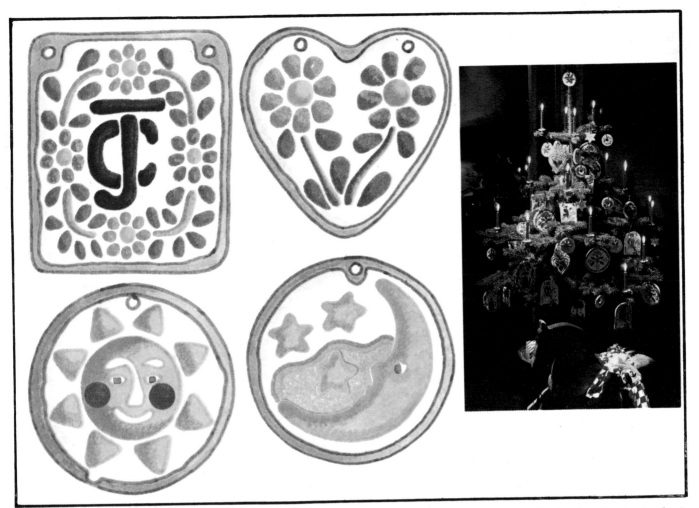

**Above left:** *Designing individual biscuits [cookies] for specific people and special occasions is lots of fun. Keep raised dough designs boldly shaped. Add details with paint brush after baking.*

**Above right:** *See what a festive display these biscuits [cookies] can make. By making a hole and threading brightly coloured cord or ribbon through, you can hang them in many delightful ways.*

Special occasions call for special food. From the cook's point of view it is certainly pleasing to create dishes that look and taste exciting, but all too often this involves expensive ingredients.

For the wise cooks of southern Germany a festive occasion means cooking a batch of special biscuits [cookies]. This is an idea well worth consideration. Baking and decorating biscuits [cookies] is fun. The results can look spectacular, enough to tempt even those who claim not to have a 'sweet-tooth' and – an added bonus – the cost of ingredients will not ruin your housekeeping budget!

The biscuits [cookies] illustrated here, a speciality of Baden-Wurttemberg, are particularly charming. Coated with royal icing and decorated with brilliantly coloured dyes, the relief design biscuits [cookies] look like painted clay tiles – and, if you make holes through them, they can be hung up to be admired just like real wall plaques.

Carefully wrapped to prevent breakage, painted tile biscuits [cookies] will keep well for a week if stored in an airtight container; if kept on display, however, they will lose their crispness and pristine looks more rapidly.

## Personalized presents

Special moulds can be bought in Germany for making these biscuits [cookies]. The moulds are not readily available in other countries but it is quite simple (and more creative) to make these delightful miniature works of art without moulds.

Your biscuits [cookies] can be unique – personally designed for the recipient. You can have fun thinking up ideas for individual people and special days. A stork carrying a baby to celebrate a christening, wreaths of holly for Christmas, romantic motifs on heart-shaped biscuits [cookies] for St. Valentine's day or an engagement party, a smiling sun face to mark the first day of summer holidays, the interwoven initials of the happy couple for a wedding party, a sign of the zodiac for a birthday are just a few ideas.

## Raised dough designs

The shortcake biscuit [cookie] recipe given is ideal for making painted tile biscuits [cookies]. If you wanted to, you could make your own clay moulds but raised surfaces can easily be obtained by decorating basic biscuit [cookie] shapes with extra dough, rolled or cut into patterns of your choice and pressed on to the biscuits [cookies] before cooking.

Butter moulds, unlike tile biscuits [cookie] moulds, can be bought in most countries and there is no reason why they should not be used to make pretty dough motifs for superimposing on basic biscuit [cookie] shapes.

33

Sprinkle the mould generously with flour then tap gently to release excess flour. Press the mould firmly into the dough and remove carefully. Dust off any flour adhering to the dough shape.

Alternatively, raised dough decorations can be made with small fondant cutters (for example to obtain really accurate crescent and star shapes).

You can also cut dough shapes with a round-bladed knife – using freehand designs or following trace pattern templates made from your own sketches or pictures taken from magazines.

You can also roll the dough in your hands to make rounded strips or little balls.

Whichever method or combination of methods you choose, it is sensible to make the biscuits [cookies] about 7.5–10cm [3–4in] across – because very small biscuits [cookies] are fiddly to decorate and can look messy rather than ornamental.

Equally it is wise to keep the dough decorations fairly simple. Very intricate relief designs (such as one or two of the German moulded figures photographed here) are complicated to execute successfully without moulds.

Roll out two-thirds of the dough until 6mm [$\frac{1}{4}$in] thick. Cut out the basic biscuit [cookie] shapes and place on

**Right:** *Take care to avoid smudging when you come to painting.*
**Below:** *Once decorated, your biscuit [cookie] is ready to be admired.*

35

**1.** *Press dough relief decorations firmly into basic biscuit [cookie] shapes before cooking. Pierce biscuits [cookies] with a skewer to have holes for threading with ribbon.*

**2.** *Cooked biscuits are left to cool on a wire rack. Do not attempt to start decorating until they are quite cold or else your decorations will not set. They will run and not look precise and definite.*

**3.** *Using a round-bladed knife or spatula give each biscuit [cookie] a smooth coat of royal icing. Leave overnight to dry. Your biscuits [cookies] are now ready to paint.*

baking trays. If you want to hang the biscuits [cookies] use a largish wooden or metal meat skewer to make a hole (or holes) in each biscuit [cookie] through which decorative ribbon or string can be threaded later. Roll out the remaining dough (this time thinner) and make your relief decorations. Use your finger on the back of a knife to press the decorations firmly into position on the biscuits [cookies].

## Painting the biscuits [cookies]

Once the cooked biscuits [cookies] are cold, extra ornamental effects can be added. First apply an overall layer of royal icing. When that has thoroughly dried (allow several hours or preferably leave overnight), there is the fun of painting on the finishing touches. This is a real chance to use your creative skills with colours.

It is of course essential to use edible dyes *not* paints to colour your biscuits [cookies]. Buy a selection of vegetable-based food dyes from your local supermarket or pharmacy, and two or more paint brushes from an art store. You will need a medium fine brush for colouring large areas and a finely tapered one for subtle shading and adding details which are too intricate to be clearly defined in dough.

Treat the biscuit [cookie] just like a canvas, dipping your brush into the dyes and painting the colours on to the thoroughly dried royal icing.

Vegetable-based food dyes usually come in fairly standard colours, but you can create your own shades by blending a drop of one colour with a drop of another. Use a saucer as your palette and experiment.

A few drops of food dye can also be stirred into a stiff royal icing for colourful piping if you want to increase the relief effect of your biscuits [cookies].

Allow the colouring to dry thoroughly before threading the biscuits [cookies] with ribbon or decorative string. Then relax and enjoy looking at, and eating your miniature works of art!

## Royal icing

| You will need: | Metric/UK | US |
|---|---|---|
| Egg white | 1/1 | 1 |
| Icing [confectioners'] sugar sifted | 175–225gm/ 6–8oz | 1½–2 cups |
| Strained lemon juice, as required. | | |

☐ Place the egg white in a medium-size bowl and beat to a foam with a wooden spoon.

☐ Add icing [confectioners'] sugar, a tablespoon at a time, beating well after each addition. Continue adding icing [confectioners'] sugar until the icing stands in firm peaks.

☐ If the icing is not required for immediate use, cover the bowl with a damp cloth to prevent a crust from forming.

☐ Just before using, stir in enough lemon juice to make a coating consistency.

**Right:** *An attractively presented selection of hand-made marzipan petits fours is a delicious after-dinner treat to delight your guests.*

# Connoisseur confectionery

Now for a really special occasion, a dinner or drinks party or perhaps a coffee morning – classic confectionery will add that final flourish.

Adult tastes are often more sophisticated than those of children and sweetmeats such as *marrons glacés*, truffles, brandy snaps and turkish delights can be very expensive to buy – but now you can concoct these mouth-watering confections and not break the bank!

Recipes for these delicacies have been treasured by traditional confectioners all over the world for centuries – and now you too can dazzle your family and friends with them. You don't have to be a connoisseur to enjoy them, though they have been enjoyed by gourmets for many years. Most of the confectionery is the perfect accompaniment to after-dinner coffee and liqueurs, though they are delicious on their own and any time you feel like eating something different.

# Marzipan

Marzipan, made by you, is so much nicer than the store-bought product. It's flavour and texture far surpasses commercial alternatives. Marzipan fruits are very decorative and fun to make as well as delicious to eat. *Petits fours* made from marzipan in the many different ways we describe will make a most attractive centrepiece, served on a silver platter with your best table linen, for dinner parties and festive occasions.

### Marzipan fruits and petits fours

The uncooked method simply involves mixing the raw ingredients together. This produces a fairly course textured marzipan suitable for moulding into *petits fours* and simply-shaped fruits.

If you wish to create life-like coloured fruits use hand-made marzipan for these sweetmeats. For top quality taste, don't buy ready-ground almonds – buy whole almonds and blanch and grind them yourself. This gives you a full flavour and oil from the nuts.

In order to keep their pristine looks, the marzipan shapes are best stored in an airtight tin and will still taste perfectly alright for 14 days or so.

### Uncooked marzipan

| You will need: | Metric/UK | US |
|---|---|---|
| Freshly ground almonds | 350gm/12oz | 2 cups |
| Icing [confectioners'] sugar, | 350gm/12oz | 2 cups |
| Castor [fine] sugar | 350gm/12oz | 2 cups |
| Small whole eggs, lightly beaten | 2/2 | 2 |
| Strained lemon juice (tablespoons) | 1–2/1–2 | 1–2 |
| Sherry (tablespoon) optional | 1/1 | 1 |
| Vanilla essence (teaspoon) | ½/½ | ½ |
| Almond essence (teaspoon) | ½/½ | ½ |

☐ Mix the almonds, castor [fine] sugar and icing [confectioners'] sugar together in a mixing bowl.
☐ Make a hollow in the centre of the dry ingredients and add the remaining ingredients.

☐ Mix well with a wooden fork, then turn on to a lightly sugared surface and knead until smooth and free from cracks.
☐ Shape immediately or wrap in polythene [plastic] and store in a cool place until ready to use.

### Fruits

Break off pieces of marzipan and colour each with a few drops of vegetable-based food dye or, for a brown colour, cocoa or gravy browning. Knead each piece of marzipan thoroughly to obtain an even blend of colouring, then roll into the desired shape.

Use a paintbrush and one colour (or a mixture of dyes) to shade the fruits and give them realistic appearances.

Peaches and plums can be given their characteristic indentation marks with the tip of a teaspoon and, when dry, brushed with icing [confectioners'] sugar for bloom. Roll strawberries and citrus fruits on a fine grater to

give them their surface pattern, then toss in a little sugar. Add stalks, leaves and strawberry hulls for finishing touches. Plastic ones can be bought from specialist confectionery shops or, if you want entirely edible fruits, make your own. Cloves make suitable stalks and calyxes for apples and pears. Slivers of angelica can be used for hulls.

Place the completed fruits on a tray and allow to harden before wrapping and storing.

## Petits fours

Prettily coloured and interestingly shaped marzipan *petits fours* are delicious to eat with after-dinner coffee. Here are a few traditional shapes, but it is fun and easy to invent your own designs and colour schemes.

**Chequers.** Divide the marzipan in two. Leave one half uncoloured and colour the other half dark brown with a little cocoa powder or gravy browning powder. Knead through to get an even colour. Make each piece into a roll about 1.25 cm [½in] in diameter. Place the rolls side by side and push firmly together to join. Cut in half and arrange one half on top of the other to give alternate colours, like a Battenberg cake. Push together firmly with a palette knife and shape into a smooth, straight-sided oblong of chequered marzipan. Then carefully cut into slices about 6mm [¼in] thick.

**Catherine wheels.** Divide the marzipan into three equal portions. Using vegetable-based food dyes which are obtainable from a pharmacy or general food store, colour one patch of marzipan bright green, the second pink and leave the third uncoloured. Roll each piece into an oblong of equal size. Place one on top of the other and press lightly with a rolling pin to seal the layers together. Trim the edges to shape if necessary then roll up tightly like a Swiss [jelly] roll. Cut into slices about 6mm [¼in] thick.

**Marbles.** Divide the marzipan into two, three or four pieces – not necessarily of equal size – and colour each differently. Shades can be contrasting or subtly blended. Lightly knead the four pieces together to obtain a swirling mixture of colours without amalgamating them. Break off small pieces and roll them into small multicoloured balls. Making marbles is an excellent way of using up marzipan trimmings.

**Stuffed dates.** Slit the dates, remove the stones and stuff the centres with plain or coloured marzipan rolled into the appropriate shape. Alternatively you can cut the dates in half to remove the stones, and sandwich them back together with marzipan. This method uses more marzipan.

**Stuffed walnuts.** Make a sandwich by pressing two walnut halves into a small oval of plain or coloured marzipan.

40

# Truffles

Popular sweets [candies] which originated in France, truffles usually have a base of chocolate which is flavoured with rum, although nuts and other spirits may be added to the chocolate. The sweets [candies] are most often ball-shaped and may be coated with chocolate vermicelli [sprinkles] or cocoa powder.

## Truffles with whisky

Truffles with whisky are surprisingly potent and they make the ideal accompaniment to strong after-dinner coffee.

| You will need: | Metric/UK | US |
|---|---|---|
| Dark [semi-sweet] cooking chocolate, melted | 175gm/6oz | |
| Egg yolk | 1/1 | 1 |

## Truffles with almonds

Rich truffles with almonds are really delicious and would make a welcome gift.

| You will need: | Metric/UK | US |
|---|---|---|
| Cocoa powder | 25gm/1oz | 4 tbsp |
| Finely chopped blanched almonds (tablespoons) | 2/2 | 2 |
| Almond essence (teaspoon) | ½/½ | ½ |
| Marzipan | 125gm/4oz | |
| **Sugar Syrup** | | |
| Sugar | 75gm/3oz | ⅜ cup |
| Water | 75gm/3fl oz | ⅜ cup |
| Vanilla essence (teaspoon) | ½/½ | ½ |

☐ First prepare the sugar syrup. Dissolve the sugar in the water in a small saucepan over moderate heat, stirring constantly.
☐ Increase the heat to high and bring the syrup to the boil. Boil the syrup until the temperature reaches 102°C [215°F] or a little syrup dropped in cold water forms a short thread.
☐ Remove the pan from the heat and set aside to cool.
☐ Meanwhile, in a medium-sized mixing bowl, add the cocoa powder, almonds and almond essence to the marzipan. Using your fingertips, mix the ingredients until they are well blended.
☐ Break off small pieces of the truffle mixture and form them into 16 balls. Dip the truffles in the sugar syrup and place them on a serving plate.
☐ Set aside to cool completely before serving.

## Truffles with rum

Possibly the most popular of all truffles, truffles with rum are easy to make and look very professional. Chocolate vermicelli [sprinkles] are tiny strands of chocolate which may be bought from most grocers.

| You will need: | Metric/UK | US |
|---|---|---|
| Dark [semi-sweet] cooking chocolate, melted | 225gm/8oz | |
| Icing [confectioners'] sugar (tablespoons) | 2/2 | 2 |
| Rum essence (teaspoons) | 1½/1½ | 1½ |
| Chocolate vermicelli [sprinkles] | 50gm/2oz | |

☐ Combine the melted chocolate, sugar and rum essence in a medium-sized mixing bowl. Using a wooden spoon, stir the mixture until the ingredients are well blended.
☐ Set the mixture aside for 15 minutes or until it has almost set. Using a teaspoon, scoop out small pieces of the mixture and, using your hands, shape them into 20 balls.
☐ Place the chocolate vermicelli [sprinkles] on a plate. Dip the balls in the vermicelli [sprinkles] to coat them completely, shaking off any excess. Place the truffles in a serving dish and serve.

## Truffles with coffee

Little sweets [candies] made with fondant, truffles with coffee are flavoured with liqueur. If you want the flavour

*A sumptuous selection of sweets [candies] flavoured with rum, nuts and other spirits that will satisfy any gourmet's palate.*

| Unsalted butter (tablespoons) cut into small pieces | 25gm/1oz | 2 |
|---|---|---|
| Icing [confectioners'] sugar, sifted (tablespoons) | 6/6 | 6 |
| Whisky (tablespoons) | 2/2 | 2 |
| Cocoa powder | 50gm/2oz | ½ cup |

☐ Combine the chocolate, egg yolk, butter, sugar and whisky in a medium-sized mixing bowl.
☐ Beat the mixture, using a wooden spoon, until the ingredients are thoroughly combined.
☐ Set the bowl aside for 25 minutes or until the mixture has almost set.
☐ Using a teaspoon, scoop out small pieces of the mixture and, using your hands, shape them into 30 cork shapes. Place the cocoa powder on a plate. Dip the cork shapes in the powder to coat them completely, shaking off the excess.
☐ Place the truffles in a serving dish and serve.

of coffee but not the expense of buying a liqueur use 1 teaspoon of instant coffee powder dissolved in 2 teaspoons of hot water instead.

| You will need: | Metric/UK | US |
|---|---|---|
| Fondant, warm | 225gm/8oz | 1 cup |
| Coffee-flavoured liqueur (tablespoon) | 1/1 | 1 |
| Light brown sugar (tablespoon) | 1/1 | 1 |
| Finely chopped blanched almonds (tablespoon) | 1/1 | 1 |
| Coconut – desiccated [shredded] | 50gm/2oz | ½ cup |

☐ Place the fondant in a medium-sized mixing bowl and sprinkle over the liqueur, sugar and almonds. Using your fingers, work all the ingredients together until the mixture is thoroughly combined.

☐ Break off small pieces of the fondant mixture and roll them into 12 balls.

☐ Place the coconut on a plate and roll the balls in it to completely coat them, shaking off any excess. Place the truffles in a serving dish and serve.

## Truffles with nuts

Quickly made sweets [candies], truffles with nuts are ideal for serving with after-dinner coffee.

| You will need: | Metric/UK | US |
|---|---|---|
| Dark [semi-sweet] cooking chocolate, broken into pieces and melted | 125gm/4oz | |
| Chopped hazelnuts finely chopped | 25gm/1oz | ¼ cup |
| Finely chopped walnuts (tablespoon) | 1/1 | 1 |
| Icing [confectioners'] sugar | 50gm/2oz | ½ cup |
| Vanilla essence (teaspoon) | ½/½ | ½ |
| Single [light] cream (tablespoon) | 1/1 | 1 |

☐ Combine the chocolate, hazelnuts, walnuts, sugar, vanilla essence and cream in a medium-sized saucepan. Stir the chocolate mixture gently, with a wooden spoon, until the ingredients are thoroughly combined.

☐ Set the bowl aside to cool for 20 minutes or until the mixture has set.

☐ Spoon small amounts of the truffle mixture out of the bowl and, using lightly oiled hands, shape the mixture into 12 balls.

☐ Place the truffles on a plate and chill in the refrigerator for 30 minutes or until they are firm. Remove the plate from the refrigerator and serve.

## Truffles with raisins

Truffles with raisins may be served as part of a selection of cakes and biscuits [cookies] or on their own.

| You will need: | Metric/UK | US |
|---|---|---|
| Condensed milk | 150ml/5fl oz | ⅝ cup |
| Cocoa powder (tablespoons) | 2/2 | 2 |
| Butter | 25gm/1oz | 2 tbsp |
| Sweet biscuits [cookies] crumbled | 50gm/2oz | ½ cup |
| Sultanas or seedless raisins | 50gm/2oz | ½ cup |

☐ Combine the milk, cocoa powder and butter in a medium-sized saucepan. Place the pan over low heat and cook, stirring constantly, until the ingredients are thoroughly combined. Increase the heat to moderate and bring the mixture to the boil, stirring constantly. Cook the mixture for 3 minutes, stirring constantly.

☐ Remove the pan from the heat and set aside for 20 minutes or until the mixture is cool but not firm.

☐ Stir in the biscuits [cookies] and the sultanas or raisins and beat well until the ingredients are thoroughly combined. Set aside to cook completely.

☐ Using a teaspoon, scoop out pieces of the mixture and, using your hands, roll them into 18 balls. Place the sweets [candies] on a serving dish and serve.

## Trucial dainties

These little sweets [candies] made with fruit and coated in chocolate are delightful to serve with after-dinner coffee. Candied kumquats may be bought from speciality food shops or from Chinese food stores.

| You will need: | Metric/UK | US |
|---|---|---|
| Dark [semi-sweet] cooking chocolate, melted | 125gm/4oz | |
| Candied kumquats | 12/12 | 12 |

☐ Place the melted chocolate in a small mixing bowl and set aside for 5 minutes or until it has thickened slightly, but not set. Pierce a kumquat with a skewer and dip it into the chocolate. Place chocolate-coated kumquat on lightly oiled greaseproof or waxed paper and set aside to cool completely. Coat the remaining kumquats in the same way.

☐ When the sweets [candies] have set, remove them from the paper and place in small paper or waxed cases.

## Marrons glacés

These luxury sweetmeats are the ideal accompaniment to sophisticated dinner parties and festive occasions served with strong after-dinner coffee or liqueurs. They also make a delicious dessert if chopped and mixed with ice-cream or covered with whipped cream.

| You will need: | Metric/UK | US |
|---|---|---|
| Chestnuts | 450gm/1 lb | |
| Vanilla sugar or castor [fine] sugar | 225gm/8oz | 1 cup |
| Glucose | 225ml/8fl oz | 1 cup |
| Water | 150ml/5fl oz | ⅝ cup |
| Vanilla essence (teaspoon) | 1/1 | 1 |

☐ Slit the chestnut skins without cutting the nuts. Place in a saucepan, cover with water and boil for 25 minutes, then peel off the skins.

☐ Place the sugar, glucose and water in a heavy-bottomed saucepan and stir over low heat until dissolved. Then

*Package your marrons glacés in many of the ways we will show you.*

42

bring the mixture to the boil.

☐ Add the chestnuts and vanilla essence (if plain sugar was used) and boil for 10 minutes.

☐ Lift out the chestnuts and place on a wire rack to drain for 24 hours.

☐ Next day bring the syrup back to the boil, add the chestnuts and simmer for 5–10 minutes until the nuts are well-coated.

☐ Lift the chestnuts onto a wire rack, and, when they are quite dry and cold transfer to an airtight container.

## Chocolate balls

Delicious melt-in-the-mouth treats which make a superb accompaniment to after-dinner coffee.

| You will need: | Metric/UK | US |
|---|---|---|
| Plain [semi-sweet] chocolate | 175gm/6oz | |
| Butter | 125gm/4oz | ½ cup |
| Egg yolks | 3/3 | 3 |
| Tablespoons sugar | 3/3 | 3 |
| Grated zest of orange (teaspoons) | 2/2 | 2 |
| Chocolate vermicelli [sprinkles] (tablespoons) | 3/3 | 3 |

☐ Soften the chocolate and butter in a small bowl over a pan of boiling water.

☐ In a separate bowl, beat the egg yolks and sugar together. Cream in the melted butter and chocolate and add the zest of orange. Place the mixture in the refrigerator until it begins to solidify but is not set hard.

☐ Occasionally moistening your hands with cold water, take small lumps of the chocolate mixture, form into ball shapes then roll them in the vermicelli [sprinkles] until coated.

## Brandy snaps

These attractive, crisp biscuits [cookies] may take a bit of time and trouble to prepare, but they are well worth the effort. Filled with brandy-flavoured cream, they may be served as a special dessert.

| You will need: | Metric/UK | US |
|---|---|---|
| Butter plus 1 tablespoon | 75gm/3oz | ⅜ cup |
| Sugar | 50gm/2oz | ¼ cup |
| Golden [light corn] syrup | 75ml/3fl oz | ⅜ cup |
| Flour | 50gm/2oz | ½ cup |
| Ground ginger (teaspoon) | 1/1 | 1 |
| Juice of ¼ a lemon | | |
| Double [heavy] cream | 175ml/6fl oz | ¾ cup |
| Brandy (tablespoons) | 2/2 | 2 |

☐ Preheat the oven to moderate Gas Mark 4, 180°C [350°F]. Grease a large baking sheet with half the tablespoon of butter. Coat the handle of a long wooden spoon with the rest of the tablespoon of butter.

☐ In a medium-sized saucepan melt the remaining butter, the sugar and golden [light corn] syrup over moderate heat. Remove the pan from the heat and beat in the flour, ginger and lemon juice. Continue beating until the mixture is smooth.

**1.** *For brandy snaps, in a medium-sized saucepan beat the flour, ginger and lemon juice into the melted butter, sugar and golden [light corn] syrup until smooth.*

**3.** *After baking in the oven, remove one brandy snap at a time from the baking sheet and curl it round a butter-coated wooden spoon handle.*

2. *Drop teaspoonfuls of the mixture onto a buttered baking sheet, leaving about a 10cm [4in] space between each teaspoonful for they expand on cooking.*

4. *Pipe the stiffly beaten cream, flavoured with brandy, into both ends of the brandy snaps. Serve these mouth-watering delights immediately for best results.*

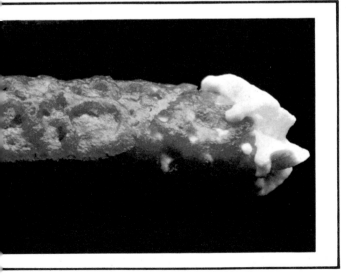

☐ Drop teaspoonfuls of the mixture on to the buttered baking sheet, leaving about 10cm[4in] between each teaspoonful.

☐ Place the baking sheet in the oven and bake for 8 to 10 minutes, or until the biscuits [cookies] are golden brown.

☐ Turn off the heat and open the oven door, but leave the biscuits [cookies] in the oven to keep them warm. If they are allowed to cool they will harden and break.

☐ With a palette knife, remove one brandy snap at a time from the baking sheet and curl it around the butter-covered spoon handle. Slide the brandy snap off the handle and on to a wire cake rack. Repeat the process with the other brandy snaps, using additional butter to coat the handle each time.

☐ Just before serving beat the cream with a wire whisk or rotary beater until it is very thick. Add the brandy and continue beating the cream until it is stiff. Fill a forcing bag with the brandied cream and pipe it into both ends of the brandy snaps. Serve at once.

## Sugared almonds

Almonds with a sugar or honey coating have been known from earliest times and were recorded as having been served in Ancient Rome at family celebrations. Hand-made sugared almonds may not look as beautiful as the commercially made variety, but they surpass them in flavour and texture. They can be stored for about a week, in an airtight jar.

| You will need: | Metric/UK | US |
|---|---|---|
| Granulated sugar | 450gm/1 lb | 2⅔ cups |
| Water | 125ml/4fl oz | ½ cup |
| Cinnamon (teaspoon) | 1/1 | 1 |
| Unblanched almonds | 450gm/1 lb | 3 cups |

☐ In a saucepan over low heat dissolve the sugar in the water stirring constantly.

☐ Add the cinnamon, stir, raise the heat and briskly boil the syrup until it falls from the spoon in thick drops. Add the almonds and stir until they are well coated.

☐ Remove the pan from the heat and continue stirring until the syrup dries into sugar.

☐ Put the almonds in a sieve and shake to dislodge the excess sugar. Put the excess sugar back in the pan, add a little water and dissolve again over a low heat. Raise heat and boil until the syrup clears. Add the almonds, stir again until the almonds are coated. Leave to cool and dry.

## Turkish delight

This eastern sweetmeat is now as popular in other countries as in its country of origin.

| You will need: | Metric/UK | US |
|---|---|---|
| Gelatine powder | 25gm/1oz | 2 tbsp |
| Water | 275ml/10fl oz | 1¼ cups |
| Rose water (teaspoon) | 1/1 | 1 |
| Sugar | 450gm/1 lb | 2⅔ cups |
| A few drops of vanilla or peppermint essence | | |
| A few drops of cochineal or | | |

edible green colouring

| | Metric/UK | US |
|---|---|---|
| Chopped nuts | 25gm/1oz | ¼ cup |
| Icing [confectioners'] sugar | 25gm/1oz | ¼ cup |
| Cornflour [cornstarch] | 25gm/1oz | ¼ cup |

☐ Lightly grease an 18–20cm [7–8in] square tin.

☐ Place gelatine powder, water, rosewater and sugar in a saucepan. Heat gently, stirring all the time, until the gelatine and sugar are completely dissolved.

☐ Increase the heat and bring to the boil, without stirring.

☐ Immediately reduce heat and leave to simmer for 20–25 minutes.

☐ Remove the pan from the heat. Stir in flavouring and colouring and leave to cool for 5 minutes.

☐ Strain the mixture into a bowl. Quickly stir in the nuts and pour into the prepared tin.

☐ Leave to set firm for 24 hours before cutting into squares.

☐ Toss the squares in mixed sieved icing [confectioners'] sugar and cornflour [cornstarch]. Pack into an airtight container, sprinkling extra sugar and flour between the layers.

## Quick crème de menthe turkish delights

These exotic sweets [candies] conjure up visions of leisure and luxury. They should be presented on a decorative paper doily on a serving plate.

| You will need: | Metric/UK | US |
|---|---|---|
| Butter (teaspoon) | 1/1 | 1 |
| Sugar | 350gm/12oz | 2 cups |
| Water | 225ml/8fl oz | 1 cup |
| Lemon juice (teaspoon) | 1/1 | 1 |
| Gelatine, dissolved in hot water | 25gm/1oz 125ml/4fl oz | ½ cup |
| Crème de menthe (tablespoon) | 1/1 | 1 |

| | | |
|---|---|---|
| Drops of green colouring | 2/2 | 2 |
| Icing [confectioners'] sugar | 50gm/2oz | ½ cup |
| Cornflour [cornstarch] | 25gm/1oz | ¼ cup |

☐ Grease a 15 x 20cm [6 x 8in] baking tin with the butter and set aside.

☐ Place the sugar, water and lemon juice in a heavy medium-sized saucepan. Place the pan over low heat and stir the mixture until the sugar has dissolved.

☐ Increase the heat to moderately high and bring the syrup to the boil. Boil the syrup until the temperature registers 126°C [260°F] on a sugar thermometer or until a little syrup dropped into cold water forms a hard ball. Remove the pan from the heat and leave it to stand for 10 minutes. Stir in the gelatine mixture, crème de menthe and green colouring and beat well, with a wooden spoon, until the mixture is evenly mixed.

☐ Pour the mixture into the greased baking tin and leave it to set in a cool place for 8 hours or overnight.

☐ Sieve the icing [confectioners'] sugar and cornflour [cornstarch] on to a working surface. Turn the turkish delight on the board and cut it into 2.5cm [1in] cubes. Toss the cubes in the sugar and cornflour [cornstarch] mixture until each cube is thoroughly coated. Serve the turkish delights immediately or wrap them in waxed paper and store in an airtight container until needed.

# Candied fruits

This is an old-fashioned way of preserving fruit in a thick sugar syrup, and while the process takes several days the preparation itself is very simple.

One can buy candied fruits in the shops, but because they are usually imported they are expensive. Made at home when the fruit is in season it is very economical. A selection in the store cupboard means you have attractive colourful decorations for sweets and puddings [desserts], additions to cakes or a sweetmeat to be served on its own after dinner.

## The fruit

Fruits used for candying should be firm and at the peak of their perfection. The firmer fruits give a more successful result than the soft fruits such as raspberries, strawberries and blackberries.

Apricots, cherries, peaches, pears, pineapple and plums are ideal and the fruits should be prepared as for cooking. Depending on the size of your bowls, it is better to prepare fruit in smaller quantities, otherwise you may find it difficult to keep topping up the syrup. Small fruits such as cherries only need stoning. Larger fruits – apricots, plums, peaches – should be peeled and then halved or quartered. It is better to candy each fruit separately, otherwise the flavour of each will be lost. Weigh the fruit and place it in a saucepan. Cover with cold water, bring to the boil and simmer until the fruit is just soft – take care not to overcook the fruit as the end result will not be so successful. Drain the fruit into a heatproof bowl and reserve the cooking water.

## Syrup

☐ For every pound of fruit make a syrup with 275ml /10fl oz [1¼ cups] of the reserved cooking water and 175gm/6oz [¾ cup] of sugar. Place the water and sugar in a heavy based saucepan, bring to the boil slowly and cook over moderate heat until a thick syrup forms.

## Candying the fruit

☐ Pour the hot syrup over the fruit (make sure it is covered with syrup) and leave for 24 hours.

☐ Every day for 3 days, drain off the syrup into a saucepan and add 50gm/2oz [¼ cup] of sugar each time. Bring to the boil and pour the syrup over the fruit.

☐ On the 5th day, drain off the syrup into a saucepan and add 75gm/3oz [⅜ cup] of sugar. Bring to the boil and when the sugar is dissolved pour over the fruit.

☐ Leave for 2 days, repeat the process and leave the fruit soaking in the syrup for 4 days.

## To dry

☐ Using a slotted spoon lift the fruit out of the syrup and spread it out on clean dry baking sheets. Leave the fruit to dry out in a very cool oven 38°C [100°F] or in a warming cupboard. Turn the fruit occasionally so it dries on all sides. It is ready when it is really dry and not sticky.

## To store

☐ Pack the fruit in wax or cardboard cartons, each layer separated by a piece of greaseproof or waxed paper. Cover with a lid or piece of paper tied round with string. It is important that the containers are not airtight, otherwise the fruit might go mouldy.

**Left:** *Turkish delight, the sweetmeat full of exotic promise.*
**Right:** *Candied fruits make a super table centrepiece.*

## Crystallized fruit

☐ This gives a sugary finish to the fruit which makes an attractive gift if packed in pretty boxes. Dip the dried candied fruit in boiling water, drain well and coat each piece of fruit with sugar.

# Fondants

## Decorated fondants

Stored in an airtight tin these attractive and easily made sweets [candies] will keep for up to two weeks. Delicious to eat with after-dinner coffee.

| You will need: | Metric/UK | US |
|---|---|---|
| Sugar | 450gm/1 lb | 2⅔ cups |
| Water | 200ml/7fl oz | ⅞ cup |

| | | |
|---|---|---|
| Cream of tartar (teaspoon) | ½/½ | ½ |
| Peppermint, vanilla, almond, orange or lemon essence (teaspoon) | ½/½ | ½ |
| Drops of food colouring of your choice | 2–4/2–4 | 2–4 |
| Decorations such as sugared voilets, roses, or mimosa balls, or nuts such as almonds or walnuts | | |

☐ Measure the sugar and water into a large heavy-gauge pan. Stir over very low heat until the sugar is completely dissolved.

☐ Then increase the heat and bring the mixture to the boil, without stirring.

☐ Sprinkle on the cream of tartar and continue boiling, without stirring, until the sugar thermometer reads 114°C–115°C [238°F–240°F] or the mixture is soft ball consistency (fig.1).

☐ Remove the pan from the heat and stir in the flavouring.

☐ Pour the fondant on to a cold, hard working surface which has been sprinkled with a little cold water. Do not scrape out any fondant which remains in the bottom of the pan.

☐ Sprinkle the surface of the fondant with a few drops of cold water and leave to cool for three minutes.

☐ Work the fondant with a spatula, bringing the mixture into the centre from the edges (fig. 2).

☐ When the fondant goes white and opaque, knead it with your hands until smooth (fig. 3).

☐ Divide the fondant in half. Sprinkle 2 drops of food colouring on one half and knead until evenly coloured (fig. 4).

☐ Flatten the mixture into a large disc shape and cut into shapes with small fondant cutters.

☐ Thoroughly wash the food colouring from your hands. Leave the rest of the mixture white or blend in 2 drops of another food colouring, then cut into shapes as before.

☐ After 1 hour, decorate the fondants with sugared flowers or nuts to complement the colourings and flavours.

## Violet creams

A classic sweet [candy] made with fondant, Violet creams taste delicious. If you cannot obtain violet essence, substitute vanilla essence.

| You will need: | Metric/UK | US |
|---|---|---|
| Fondant | 450gm/1 lb | 2 cups |
| Drops of purple food colouring | 4/4 | 4 |
| Violet essence (teaspoon) | ¼/¼ | ¼ |
| Crystallized Violets | 24/24 | 24 |

☐ Place the fondant on a working surface. Using the heel of your hand, knead the colouring and essence into the fondant until the colouring is evenly distributed.

☐ Break off small pieces of the fondant and shape them into balls. Press a crystallized violet on top of each fondant ball.

☐ Set aside to harden for 1 hour. Place the violet creams in little paper cases and store in an airtight tin until required.

Fig. 1 *Test the consistency by dropping a teaspoon of it into a dish of cold water.*

Fig. 2 *Work the cooled fondant until it turns white and opaque.*

Fig. 3 *Knead the fondant thoroughly to make it completely smooth and pliable.*

Fig. 4 *Knead in colouring and cut into shapes.*

# Boxes and bows

Most of the sweets [candies] and confectionery you have made will have been for your own pleasure and indulgence, but some you will want to give as presents to your friends and family. Hand-made sweets [candies] are a suitable present for any occasion. Simple or lavish, sweets [candies] made by you, decorated and presented attractively will say 'thank you' or 'I love you' in a much more personalized way than store-bought sweets [candies] and confectionery. Fresh ingredients, imagination and careful cooking will create original and special flavoured delicacies – a delight for adults as well as children.

The gift of hand-made goodies, however, is not the only pleasure, for the container will last as a pretty memento long after the food has been eaten. Presentation is as necessary as the contents to make any food gift a highly appreciated treat. These sweets [candies] attractively presented will not only make them look more inviting but also will keep the sweets [candies] and confectionery in good condition. Cling film, waxed and non-stick papers are most effective as they keep sweets [candies] really airtight. If you give these wrappers decorative finishing touches by covering them with tinfoil, gold, silver, brightly coloured or patterned – you will enhance their looks.

Making your own boxes and bows will convince your friends that you have hidden talents. We will show you how to make boxes of all shapes and sizes, round, square, oval, petal and cone-shaped for the different varieties of sweets [candies] and confectionery you will have made. Ribbon bows or perhaps even a spray of flowers will add the finishing touch to a present made by you. We will show you how to make your own bows as well as giving you other suggestions on how to present your sweets [candies].

## Making your own boxes

### Scoring

Most heavy paper and cardboard is made up of layers, rather like a sandwich. The aim of scoring is to cut through one of the outer 'bread' layers, leaving the rest intact (fig. 1).

Once the cardboard has been scored it can be bent accurately and this is the essential technique to learn when making boxes.

**To score,** mark the line to be cut in pencil, then, draw along the line lightly with a razor-sharp cutting tool,

such as a scalpel, against a metal ruler. Be sure to keep your fingers behind the cutting blade.

If too much pressure is put on the cutting tool and you have cut too deeply, the cardboard will simply divide in two. On the other hand if the cardboard is scored too lightly, it will not bend successfully.

A little experimentation will soon reveal how much pressure to use with different sorts of cardboard.

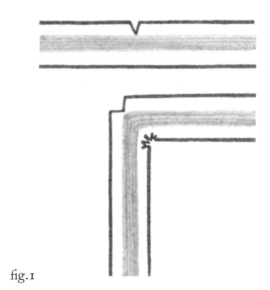

fig. 1

### Suitable cardboards

Boxes can be constructed out of varying thicknesses of cardboard, depending on the type and size you are making. Small boxes with flaps should be made of cardboard about the thickness of a cereal packet. Thick cardboard, such as mounting board, is not recommended for boxes with flaps, because the flaps tend to drop off quickly, being attached only by a thin scored layer of cardboard.

If using thick cardboard with a coloured surface for a box without flaps the scored lines will show white, so use the type which is coloured throughout unless the box is to be covered on completion.

You can begin making boxes out of any stiff paper or cardboard to hand, but there are many suitable cardboards on the market which will probably make a better job of it.

Different suppliers have different names for their

**Above:** *How to bend and score your cardboard.*
**Left:** *A delightful display of the packaged sweets* [candies].

products. There are many different good quality cardboards suitable for small boxes. Some coloured throughout, and they come in a wide variety of shades and go up to thicknesses of about 3mm [⅛in].
Other types come in pale colours, in two thicknesses.
White card is also available in sheets of about 570mm x 725mm [about 22 x 29in].
Check what types of cardboard your local art suppliers has and choose from them.

## Glues
When it comes to sticking boxes together, PVA Wood adhesive is recommended for working with cardboard, and rubber solution is the best thing for sticking down paper coverings. There are several animal-based glues on the market which are designed especially for paper work. A thick mixture of wallpaper paste can also be used for sticking heavy wallpaper coverings, but it will cause bubbles to form on thin paper and can make the cardboard bubble if it is too liquid.

## Making the boxes

### You will need:

Steel ruler
White or coloured cardboard
Animal glue or wood adhesive
Rubber solution adhesive
Scalpel or sharp cutting tool
Various types of adhesive tape
A pair of compasses [compass]
Assortment of fancy papers
Coloured pencils

## One piece boxes
☐ In this type of box, the lid is virtually an extended flap. Draw the pattern in fig.2 with all squares equal in size. Draw round a square object to create a square to make sure all angles are 90°.

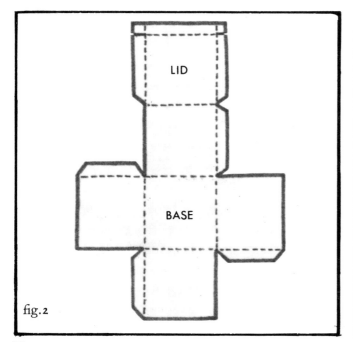

fig.2

☐ Cut along solid lines; score along dotted lines. Fold and stick as in fig.3a and b.
☐ This pattern can be easily adapted to other proportions (fig.3c). The main point to remember is that the sides must all be the same depth and the lid must match the base.

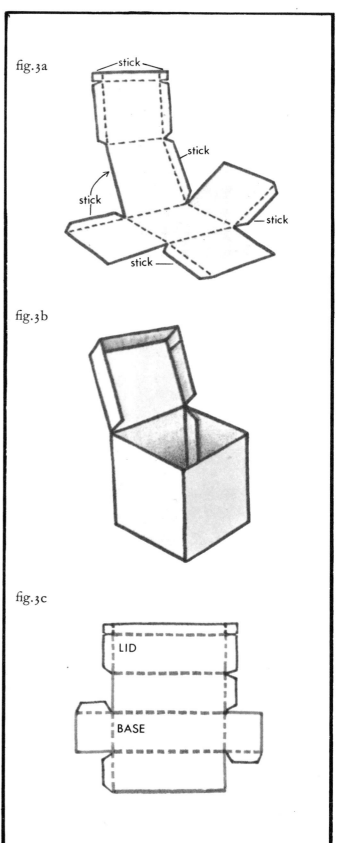

fig.3a

fig.3b

fig.3c

## A simple box

☐ To make the box cut a 36cm [14in] square of paper. Fold the diagonals, open out and then fold the corners into the centre (fig.1). Open out. You now have a square folded diagonally within the paper square.

☐ Now fold each corner to the far side of the inner square (fig.2). Finally, fold each corner to the near side of the inner square (fig.3).

☐ On one corner, make cuts two squares deep on either side of the centre fold (fig.3). Do the same on the corner opposite this.

☐ Fold the two sides without cuts inwards along existing creases (fig.4). Fold over the ends of these sides again. Fold the remaining two corners along existing creases and slot the ends under the ends of the previous two sides (fig.5). This completes the box.

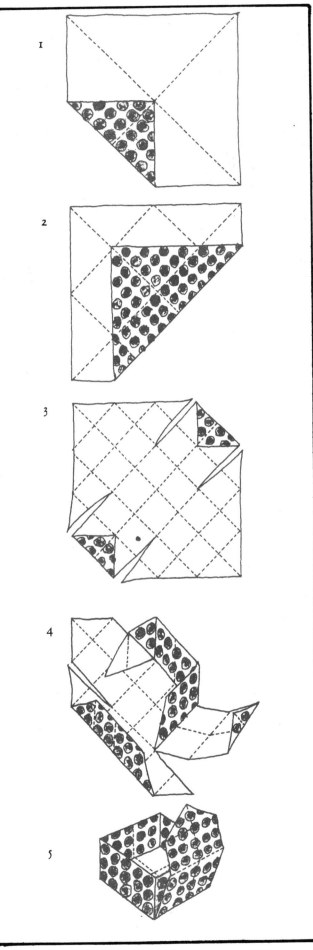

## Boxes with separate flapped lids

Make a separate lid by cutting the pattern as in fig.1. Cut along solid lines; score along dotted lines. Draw the centre square 1.6mm [$\frac{1}{16}$in] larger all round than base of the box so that the lid will fit over it. Stick flaps inside lid.

**Covering boxes.** If attractive cardboard is not available you can use something easily obtainable such as a cornflake packet and cover it in attractive wrapping paper. When covering boxes with decorative papers, remember not to stick the covering to the flap areas, or it will make the joins too bulky.

Stick the covering to the box while it is still flat and assemble the box while the covering paper is still damp, when it will have more give.

Draw your own shapes, patterns and designs like the butterfly illustrated and trace them on to the box you have made to make them bright and gay.

*Brightly coloured cards pasted with cheerful wrapping papers have been used for these easy-to-make petal boxes in which to present the sweets [candies].*

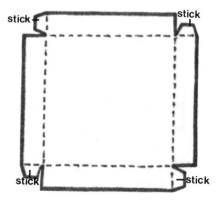

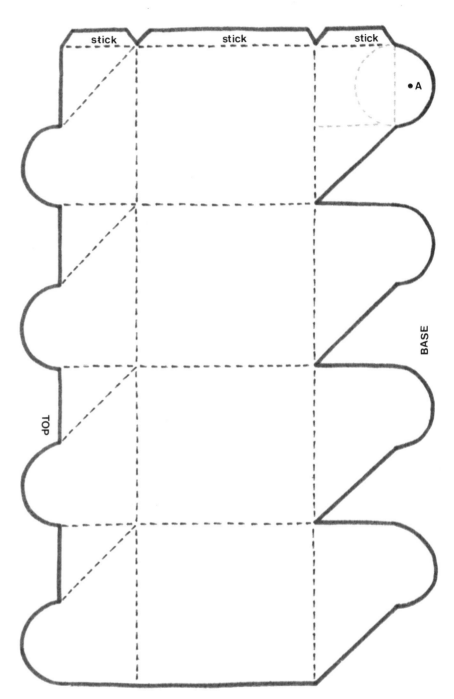

stick     stick     stick

• A

TOP

BASE

*Butterfly motif to paste onto the lid or sides of your box.*

## Petal boxes

These charming little boxes with four petal tops and bottoms need the minimum of sticking because most of the flaps tuck neatly into one another. They are easy to make.

Make them out of coloured or white cardboard and decorate them with lighthearted gummed paper motifs, cut-outs from magazines, stars, spangles, sequins or anything else you can think of.

The pattern given is for a box measuring about 9cm x 7.8cm x 7.8cm [3½ x 3 x 3in] square. To make your own size box, keep these proportions but double or treble the measurements, or reduce them by half.

### You will need:

Rough paper for pattern

55

Thin cardboard measuring about 22cm x 32cm [8½ x 12in]
Pair of compasses [compass]
Ruler
Pencil
Scalpel
Cutting board
Paper adhesive

---

□ Following fig.2 cut out a trial paper pattern of rough paper first, as this will save precious cardboard.
□ Draw the figure to the measurements shown, lightly indicating scoring lines. To make accurate circular tabs, draw a square, the sides of which measure half the length of the top of one of the sides of the box (fig. 2). Point A is half-way along one of the sides of that square as shown. Draw a circle from point A, with its radius half the length of the sides of that square.
□ Score lightly along the orange dotted lines from underneath because they are valley or sunken folds, and score lightly along the brown dotted lines from above because they are mountain or peak folds.
□ Fold to form the box, sticking at the sticking tabs.
□ Fold down the top and bottom of the box. Stick the base.

## To make round boxes

With a pair of compasses [compass], draw a circle on cardboard to make the bottom of the box.
With the same centre draw in another circle with a radius 1.3cm [½in] wider than the first one.

Cut a straight piece of cardboard the length of the circumference of the inner circle, plus a 1.3cm [½in] overlap, and the height you want the box to be.

Overlap the sides and stick them together to make a cylinder.

**To make a base** if using thick cardboard, score on the dotted inner line of the base circle and cut on the solid outer line as shown in fig.1.
Snip into the outer circle and remove alternate segments to make tabs as shown. Bend tabs upwards and stick to the base of the cylinder with the tabs inside the body of the box.
If using thinner cardboard, the base can be V-notched (fig.2).

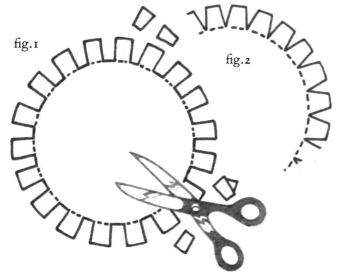

fig.1    fig.2

**Make the lid** the same way as the base, but draw the inner circle 15mm [⅜in] wider in radius. Make the side of the lid about 1.3cm [½in] deep.

## Covering round boxes

Wallpaper is suitable for covering round boxes. It comes in hundreds of attractive designs and colours and will also add strength to the box. But wallpaper will not bend sharply and should therefore be butted at the side joins and cut right up to the top and bottom edges of the box.
Most thinner paper will bend easily, so when using them cut a circle of paper the same size as the box base with an additional 1.3cm [½in] margin all round. Cut tabs 1.3cm [½in] into the circle, stick the circle to the bottom of the box, then turn up the overlapping tabs and stick them all round the sides to the box.
Cut a strip of paper the length of the circumference of the box with a 1.3cm [½in] overlap. For the depth you can add an extra 1.3cm [½in] for turning over the top edge to the inside of the box or you can cut it to the top of the box only. Stick round the sides of the box covering the turned-up tabs of the base.

## Oval boxes

Make these in the same way as round boxes – draw around an oval shape to obtain a pattern.

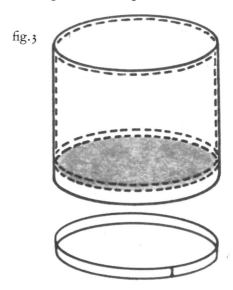

fig.3

*Dotted lines indicate lining card used to make a stronger box. The lining rim is the same diameter as the base.*

## Lining boxes

Boxes can be given an inner cardboard lining to make a recessed base and to make a stronger box.
Make up the outer cylinder as before, but do not add the base yet.
Cut the lining card 6mm [¼in] shorter and 3mm [⅛in] narrower than the outer cylinder. Bend into a cylinder, stick and then slide it in inside the outer box, leaving 6mm [¼in] at the bottom (fig.3). Cut the base circle of card the same diameter as the outer shell. Push this base circle up into the outer cylinder until it is stopped by the lining cylinder. Hold the base circle in place by sticking a circular lining rim of card 6mm [¼in] deep inside the outer cylinder. The base is now firmly sandwiched between the lining cylinder and the lining rim.

# Bows to make

Ready tied bows are available in different styles and colours – here are some to make for yourself. Use commercial self-adhesive ribbon, or use glue or transparent tape that is sticky on both sides.

## Simplicity

Loop both ends of a short piece of ribbon. Moisten and attach (diagram 1). Wrap a very short piece around the centre and moisten or glue it securely (diagram 2).

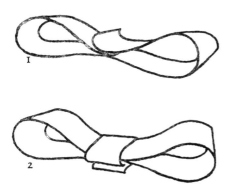

## Figure eight bow

For a 17.5cm [7in] bow, cut a 1 metre 23cm [4ft] length of ribbon. Form a figure eight with one end. Moisten or glue and attach at the centre (diagram 1). Make another figure eight, a little smaller than the first, on top. Continue until you come to the end of the ribbon (diagram 2). Wrap a short piece of ribbon around the centre of the bow. Moisten or glue it securely (diagram 3).

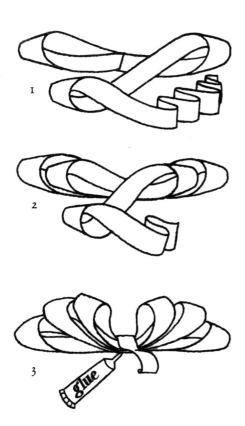

## Star bow

Make a knotless bow, using 2cm [$\frac{7}{8}$in] or wider ribbon. Give each loop a half twist, fastening it underneath (diagram 1). Loops will look like figure eights (diagram 2). Repeat the process until you have six pairs, and attach diagonally. To make a variation of this use two colours or ribbon (diagram 3).

## Knotless bow

For a 12.5cm [5in] bow, cut 12 strips of ribbon 27.5cm [11in] long. Moisten or glue both ends of one piece and press to the centre (diagram 1). Make another bow and attach it to the one you have already made (diagram 2). Repeat until you have six pairs. Moisten or glue the pairs one by one, and attach them diagonally (diagram 3).

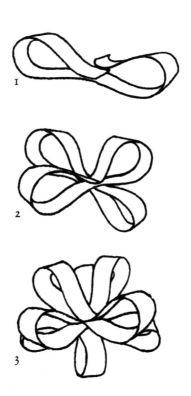

# More bows

## Spaghetti bow

For a 12.5cm [5in] bow cut a 1cm [⅜in] wide piece of ribbon into 14 pieces each 40cm [16in] long. Make a figure '8' from each piece. Moisten or glue and secure at the centre (fig.1). Moisten or glue and attach one figure '8' crosswise at the centre of another (fig.2). Continue attaching figure '8's until bow is complete (fig.3).

## Butterfly bow

Pinch six ribbon circles into oval shapes (fig.1). Moisten and attach the six ovals at one end to form wings. Make up three others. Cut body from black ribbon (fig.2).

Cut a strip of ribbon approximately 15cm [6in] long for antennae. Fold in centre and form rings at both ends (fig.3). Attach wings and antennae to body of butterfly shown in fig.4.

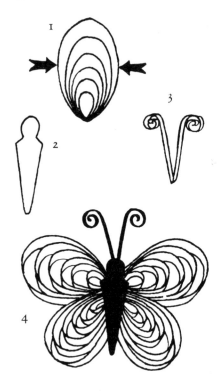

## Swirl bow

Criss-cross four pieces of 28cm [11in] ribbon and stick together (fig.1). Join the ends of each piece of ribbon to form a ball shape (fig.2). Moisten the inside centre of the criss-cross. Twist the top a quarter turn and press firmly to the bottom (fig.3).

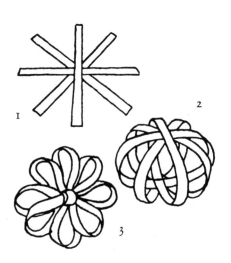

## Sunburst bow

Make a knotless bow (already given). With sharp scissors, snip two slashes (from opposite directions) into the outer edge of each loop (fig.5).

*From left to right: Here we have illustrated some of the bows we have shown you how to make. With a little imagination you can see how striking you can make them by combining and contrasting different colours you can use both ordinary ribbon and any of the commercial brands available which are already adhesive, requiring only a damp sponge to make one piece stick to another in any way you choose.*

**1st row**: *A swirl, a butterfly and a clover leaf variation on the butterfly bow.*

**2nd row**: *Some colourful butterfly bows.*

**3rd row**: *A swirl bow with a simple at the centre followed by two sunburst bows.*

# Wrap it up

Wrapping round and oval boxes or tubes is an art in itself and can be a little daunting if you don't know how to go about it, but there are several attractive ways of tackling the problem.

## Round and oval boxes

**Using wrapping paper.** Trace the top and bottom of the box or cylinder and cut out two circles (fig.1).

### Fig. 1

Wrap the sides of the box, trimming the overlap so that it can be turned slightly (fig.2). Secure with concealed tape.

### Fig. 2

Trim the ends so that the paper extends slightly over the top and bottom of the box. Snip into the edges of the wrapping paper up to the edges of the box (fig.3). Secure with paste or tape.

### Fig. 3

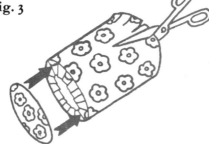

Attach the circles to the top and bottom of the box with paste or concealed tape (fig.3).

**With tissue paper** follow the same method but cut the top and bottom circles out of card and cover these with tissue paper.

To do this, cut two slightly larger circles of tissue paper, snip into the edges of the paper up to the edges of the cardboard circles and turn the tissue paper under. Glue the circles to the top and bottom of the box. This prevents the glue showing through.

## Cylinders and tubes

Wrap the paper around two or three times. Tie the ends like a cracker with ribbon or tie and flare the ends of the completed gift wrap or fringe them (fig.4).

**Fig. 4**

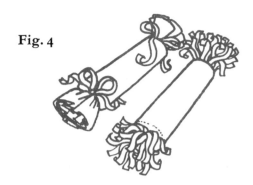

*These pastel coloured, round parcels demonstrate the two different ways of wrapping, with pleats or with end circles.*

**Pleated ends.** Leave an overlap at both ends of the cylinder to tube, the length of which should be about the length of the radius of the circle. Fold pleats towards the centre of the circle and when the last fold is in place, seal the centre of the circle with a decorative seal or bow. The thinner the paper, the smaller the pleats can be and the more professional your parcel will look.

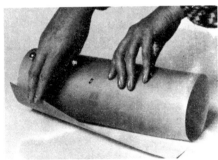

**1.** *Leave an overlap at both ends of parcel.*

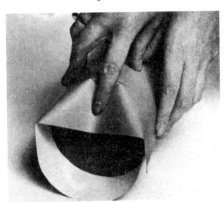

**2.** *Start folding overlap towards centre.*

**3.** *Turn parcel and fold again to centre.*

**4.** *Seal centre of pleats after last fold.*

# More ideas for presents

Depending on the occasion or who the present is for, you can pack sweets or candies into all sorts of unusual containers. Glass jars, stoneware pots, straw baskets, mugs or jugs, egg cups and flower pots are a few ideas that you could use as containers that will not only be much appreciated and useful, but also attractive after the contents have been eaten. In this way, you will be able to give two presents in one!

At Easter time, you can fill cardboard eggs with your own hand-made sweets [candies]. At Christmas, fill 'crackers' made from the decorated empty cardboard tubes of paper towel or toilet paper with an assortment of sweets [candies] and confectionery for a novel gift. Children will love to have their goodies put in cone-shaped containers made from brightly striped paper or coloured foil. You could also make a fringed pouch with circles of paper. Use two or three layers of different colours, put sweets [candies] in the middle, gather up the edges and tie the sweets [candies] in with coloured ribbons. Snip the top of the paper to make a fringe. You could turn the fringed pouch into a face by sticking coloured shapes of paper onto the pouch to represent eyes, nose, and mouth – the fringe will represent the hair. With a little imagination and minimal expenditure you can make use of existing containers and materials you

**Above:** *The gift of hand-made candies is not the only delight, for the container such as unusual glass jars, perspex boxes or stacking jars will last long after the candies have been eaten and will be much appreciated.*

**Right:** *A glass storage jar with a fitted glass lid crammed full of goodies makes a lovely gift.*

**Far right:** *Cone-shaped containers filled with everybody's favourites like fudge, brandy snaps, peppermint creams, chocolate balls and sugared almonds makes a treat for festive occasions.*

have to create pretty packaging. Spray paints, nail varnish, stick-on coloured shapes, scraps of felt or left-over wallpaper can be used to cover trade marks and give colour to your packaging. You can add a touch of originality by glueing shells or dried flowers or the bows we have shown you how to make, to cork stoppers. Paper lace doilies can also give new life to old jars and containers. Beautifully hand-scripted ornate lettering on coloured stick-on labels, or professional-looking black and gold transfer letters can give the final personal touch to a gift.

The individual sweets [candies] can be covered in foil, waxed paper or twists of transparent paper. Others can be decorated with nuts, mimosa balls, silver dragées or crystallized flowers and petals.

To make your crystallized flowers and petals, choose violets, primroses, fruit blossom and marigold petals for a bright splash of colour. If you use other flowers, make sure that they are not poisonous. Put 25gm [1oz] of gum arabic in a bowl, cover it with triple strength rose-water and leave for 24 hours. When the gum arabic has melted, using a fine paintbrush, carefully paint over each flower or petal. Make sure the petals are completely coated on both sides. Sprinkle castor [fine] sugar thoroughly all over them. Allow them to dry, and then store them carefully on layers of greaseproof paper.

So you can see that there are countless ways of making your sweets [candies] and confectionery look interesting and presentable if you use a little imagination. These are only a few ideas – no doubt you will be able to think of many more yourself.

# Index